The Worker Grows Old

Poverty and Isolation in the City

THE
WORKER
GROWS
OLD

george s. rosenberg

Jossey-Bass Inc., Publishers
615 Montgomery Street · San Francisco · 1970

THE WORKER GROWS OLD
Poverty and Isolation in the City
George S. Rosenberg

Jossey-Bass, Inc., Publishers
615 Montgomery Street
San Francisco, California 94111

Library of Congress Catalog Card Number 78-110628
Standard Book Number SBN 87589-053-9

Manufactured in the United States of America
Composed and printed by York Composition Co., Inc.
Bound by Chas. H. Bohn & Co., Inc., New York

JACKET DESIGN BY WILLI BAUM, SAN FRANCISCO

FIRST EDITION

Code 7004

THE JOSSEY-BASS BEHAVIORAL SCIENCE SERIES

General Editors

WILLIAM E. HENRY
University of Chicago

NEVITT SANFORD
Wright Institute, Berkeley

Special Adviser in Adult Development

MARJORIE FISKE LOWENTHAL
Langley-Porter Neuropsychiatric Institute, San Francisco

26986

Preface

The interest directly responsible for *The Worker Grows Old* has its roots in the study of social stratification. I have been examining a theoretical problem which has a long history in social thought, namely, how to account for the social isolation of the working class. Although this is a problem of many dimensions, primary and secondary social participation are generally recognized as crucial. An important series of investigations, discussed in the chapters to follow, have attempted to describe these patterns of social participation in the working class. I have been concerned with the lack of clarity in information about the bases of working class social participation with friends and kin, and hence with the seemingly premature character of comparisons often made between working and middle class patterns of social interaction. During the course of my examination of this research, I noticed, in particular, how much of our knowledge depended on data about young adults. In the subsequent search for some material on patterns of social participation among middle-aged and older people, I was inevitably led to theories and controversies concerning the isolation of the aged. It became apparent at once that theories articulated in terms of gerontology and stratification were offering contradictory explanations for this phenomenon of social isolation. The substantial difference in the empirical base of our knowledge about working class social isolation had yielded a dilemma. This led to the work reported in *The Worker Grows Old*.

When the plan of this study was conceived, only a few years ago, comparatively little notice was taken of older people in American society beyond the recognition that they constituted a social problem, were the proper object of a somewhat melioristic public policy, and were the subject of a small interdisciplinary field, gerontology. A number of conditions undoubtedly could have explained the relative lack of social science research on older segments of the population. Not the least of these conditions was the scarcity of funds for investigation of the social aspects of the lives of older people. But also, the small amount of attention devoted to older cohorts in our society fit well with some dominant

American outlooks, especially our admiration for those who could remain active, independent, and self-sufficient; our high valuation of youth; and our stress on the struggles of achievement, which we tend to define for the most part as occurring in late adolescence and early adulthood. Origins, beginnings, and early development receive the lion's share of emphasis in our culture. Later maturation, destinations, and endings tend to be swept under the rug. Even our similes and metaphors depicting old age seize on the decrements of physiological functioning to convey an image of decline, if not waste.

Recently, however, there has been something of a change. Both social researchers and those who formulate public policy have discovered the aged. To be sure, this attention does not indicate a major shift in values. Rather, practical considerations have placed the aged in sharper contrast to the younger population. The number and proportion of the population over age sixty-five have grown steadily and give every indication of continuing to do so. By virtue of size, the older elements in the population have become a more powerful force in the electorate than they were before, and have begun to form the rudiments of political pressure groups. Present and predicted shortages of certain skills and talents have led to a redefinition of some of the retired labor force as a labor reserve. Medical and scientific advances have held out the promise of prolonging life considerably beyond present expectations. And perhaps most important of all, in the latest of the many rediscoveries of the poor in our midst which we as a nation have made, it has been "found" that the aged contribute substantially to the dimensions of the poverty problem. Along with these developments, we are now seeing, and hope to see increasingly in the future, a growth in knowledge about age grading in our society and about the impact of age-related changes on the social roles of older people.

In carrying out this study, I have become indebted to many people and organizations for aid and advice. This work was initially made possible by partial support from the Social Security Administration and the Welfare Administration, United States Department of Health, Education and Welfare (grants 193(1)-5-127 and 193(2)-6-187). Analysis of the data which appears in Chapter Six was supported by a National Science Foundation institutional fund administered by Case Western Reserve University. Thanks are due to the editor of the *Journal of Gerontology* for permission to use material which appeared there in an article of mine.

I received wise counsel on both methodological and substantive aspects of this study from Herbert H. Hyman and Philip C. Sagi. I owe a special debt of gratitude to Morris Rosenberg for his careful reading of an early draft of the manuscript and for his incisive criticisms and suggestions. My student Donald Frederick Anspach has contributed to the perspective on family and kinship studies in Chapter Five.

I wish to thank Aaron Spector for guidance and assistance at every stage of the field work of this study in Philadelphia. Ellen Michelson, who served as field supervisor, and a staff of more than fifty professional interviewers deserve admiration as well as gratitude for performance of a difficult task.

I am grateful also to Fred Meier, Samuel Lyerly, Richard Jones, John Kert, and Joseph Cocozza, who rendered assistance at various stages of this study. And for preparing the manuscript for publication, I wish to thank Pat Howard.

My wife's contributions to this work have been indirect but indispensable.

The Worker Grows Old is dedicated to my parents, David and Sadie Rosenberg.

GEORGE S. ROSENBERG

Cleveland Heights, Ohio
February, 1970

Contents

xiii

The Worker Grows Old

Poverty and Isolation in the City

CHAPTER 1

Social Isolation of the Working Class

True earnest sorrows, rooted miseries,
Anguish in grain, vexations ripe and blown,
Sure-footed griefs, solid calamities,
Plain demonstrations, evident and cleare,
Fetching their proofs ev'n from the very bone;
 These are the sorrows here.

GEORGE HERBERT
Dotage

1

he Worker Grows Old explores the relationships between poverty and old age and between poverty and social isolation from friends and kin. Our subjects are a sample of white working class Philadelphians between the ages of forty-five and seventy-nine. We compare the friendship and kinship relations of these aged and middle-aged people who are poor with similar relations of their solvent counterparts. And we investigate some of their attitudes and beliefs which bear on isolation, old age, and social class position.

An apparent dilemma confronting those who would study working class social isolation arises from the existence of two orientations toward the problem of isolation. These orientations, by and large, have remained independent of each other; they stem from research on aging and research on social stratification.

Gerontologists such as Rosow (1962) point out that certain institutional conditions which have served in the past to integrate the aged socially—such as their control of property, opportunities, and strategic knowledge and skills; the low-productivity economy; and the high mutual dependence among members of a society, especially among families—are rapidly being eroded in the United States. A trend toward the isolation of the elderly through the loss of social roles and of group memberships has become clear. Changes in familial and employment roles and decline in health, income, participation in formal organizations, and also, to some extent, participation in informal associations tend to weaken the social relationships of the aged. As older persons become less socially visible, they become less a source of concern. Their retirement from work, their decreasing family authority, and their lower income, all weaken their claim to consideration from others, and they become increasingly detached. In the most extreme cases, they may become, in Townsend's (1957) term, "desolates," devoid of social contact. A corollary view held by some gerontologists—for example, Cumming, Dean, Newell, and McCaffrey (1960), and Cumming and Henry (1961)—regards aging as a mutual withdrawal of the aged person and others around him—a process which, it is claimed, is intrinsic to the late stages of the life cycle and which constitutes

2

the modal pattern of adjustment of the aged. This claim is based
on a sample which Cumming and Henry (1961, p. 27) chose
"from a population of physically healthy adults who had no major
economic worries."

But students of social stratification note that social isolation
is also associated with low status or with poverty. Knupfer's (1947)
old but not entirely outdated synthesis of knowledge about lower
class social participation points out the limited nature of informal
social interaction, especially among friends, in the lower class. And
a more recent critique by Blum (1964) challenges the traditional
impression that family interaction is more extensive and intensive
the lower one descends in the class hierarchy. In fact, not only can
evidence be cited for just the opposite conclusion, but also past
impressions of greater working class integration among extended kin
have been questioned by Blum (1964, p. 204) as artifacts of
geographical propinquity and social mobility.

Thus, gerontological research associates social isolation with
aging, while the stratification tradition associates it with low social
standing or poverty. Yet the presence of many poor among the
aged, including some who have been poor for the greater part of
their lives, leads us to question whether it is mainly poverty or
aging or both which are responsible for social isolation. Does
economic deprivation or a history of economic deprivation contribute more to the social isolation of the aging poor than does loss
of occupational ties and familial roles? Does loss of roles and group
memberships contribute more to isolation among the aging solvent
working class than does lack of income, or do higher rates of interaction during their working years act as a cushion on retirement?

THE EVIDENCE

Empirical studies of the working class which may be
marshaled to present a coherent picture of working class isolation
are contradictory at times and scant in any case. Nevertheless,
several studies of the variations in both family and nonfamily
interaction form a basis for departure.

Much evidence supports the view that the operative kinship system in American society extends beyond the nuclear family.
Litwak (1960a, 1960b) found no break in kin ties due to either

geographic or social mobility, although Hollingshead (1955) suggests that close kinship ties are often broken in the mobility process.
Cumming and Schneider (1961) found that their respondents
could name a median of 151 kin and that at least half of these
recognized kin were known to the respondent personally. And
studies by Axelrod (1956), Survey Research Center (1957), Greer
(1956), Leichter and Rogers (1963), and Shanas and Streib
(1965) suggest a fairly high frequency of social contact and participation with relatives.

Despite this evidence, there is an important lack of information on social class variations in family interaction. Most
relevant research has been confined to middle class populations,
and relatively little attention has been paid to the lower class, much
less to families in poverty. Bell and Boat (1957) found that "family
status" (social rank) and economic position were both correlated
with frequency of social participation with relatives. Slightly greater
proportions of adult males in neighborhoods of low economic status
than of those in higher status areas had never had contact with
relatives or saw them only about once a year. On the other hand,
Cohen and Hodges (1963, especially p. 310) found that lower
blue-collar subjects interacted more with relatives both absolutely
and also relative to their interaction with friends and neighbors than
did upper lower class and middle class subjects. Comparison of
data gathered by Shanas (1961a), Young and Geertz (1961),
Litwak (1960a, 1960b), Sussman (1953, 1959), and Willmott
and Young (1960, Ch. VII) suggests only a moderate association,
if any, between socioeconomic level and frequency of interaction
with relatives. Within the working class, Pope (1964) found, a
history of cumulative economic deprivation was inversely related to
informal association with kin other than those living in the same
household. He suggests that "restriction of contact with relatives
is a permanent correlate of economic deprivation persisting far
beyond the episodes of job loss" (p. 298).

These studies do not allow definitive conclusions about the
relationship of class to family interaction and its bearing upon
social isolation. Whether there is a differential in sheer frequency
of interaction among extended family members in different social
classes is unclear. And we have no evidence of the universality of

a modified extended kinship arrangement among all levels of the
social class hierarchy. Therefore, whether such an arrangement exists
in the solvent working class or among those in poverty is a question we
address in this study. We hope to shed some light on it, if only
inferentially, by noting whether differential rates of interaction
with kin exist among poor and solvent working class people of
middle and old age.

Research on the family interaction of the aged has been
concentrated on the relationship between two generations in the
family. Sussman (1959) found that residential mobility was common on an extended family basis, especially in the working class,
and Shanas (1961b) and Young and Geertz (1961) account
for the migration of old people by their desire to live near an adult
child. Mutual aid between generations has been found by Sussman
(1953) to continue after children reach adulthood, and Shanas
(1961a), Schorr (1960), and Kaplan (1957) have shown the
substantial extent to which adult children have provided for their
parents' needs, including the provision of a home. Furthermore,
responsibility for aged parents seems to be strongly associated with
working class status as indicated by Stone and Slocum (1957) and
Townsend (1957); here, for example, the older generation contributed child care service, enabling a mother to work.

Also, a finding by Lowenthal (1964) deserves mention here,
even though the measure of isolation included nonfamily as well as
family contacts. She suggests that most of the extreme isolates among
samples of hospitalized and nonhospitalized aged were always that
way. Elaboration of this finding was not possible because the nonhospitalized sample yielded only thirty isolates, and supplementary
data were scarce since the focus of the study was elsewhere.

The bulk of these studies seems to point to the conclusion
that intergenerational family interaction continues at a fairly steady
rate into old age. Still, we do not have systematic data comparing
old and young, poor and solvent, with respect to their interaction
with all primary and secondary kin. And, importantly, we have no
estimates on the role played by propinquity, genealogical distance,
and the size of the kin network in the interaction of older people
with their families. We consider these matters later in this study.

Little research has been done on friendship in old age. Some findings—for instance, Dean (1962)—suggest that friendships become shallower with age. Several studies indicate that members of the working class rely more than do members of the middle class on their immediate environment for friends. Bell (1957), Bell and Boat (1957), and Smith, Form, and Stone (1954) found that neighbors were the major source of friends for the working class but that this source was not nearly so important to the middle class. With age, according to Axelrod (1956), Dotson (1951), and Dubin (1956), in all social strata informal relationships among friends and neighbors become more important than does formal social participation. But little is known about the relative degree of reliance upon neighbors for friendship among those in poverty, in the solvent working class, and in the middle class as the role losses which accompany aging increase. Blau (1961) suggests that the extent to which friendships form after old people lose spouses depends upon the prevalence of others with similar losses in the neighborhood. But this finding was true for the middle and not for the lower classes in her sample.

These studies imply that working class isolation from friends may be related to the availability of others of like age and economic standing. What differentials in isolation exist between the poor and the solvent and the aged and the middle aged in areas with various degrees of opportunity for association with peers is not known however. We pursue this question in the next chapter.

THE SAMPLE

Studying poverty and aging as factors in social isolation calls for a sample of a white working class population which permits comparisons between poor and solvent blue-collar people and between the middle aged and the aged. Poverty was defined in this study by a variable family income criterion, depending upon family size. A family income of $7,500 per year from all sources was the upper limit of solvency. And the sample was restricted to persons between forty-five and seventy-nine in households where the head was employed as a blue-collar worker or, if retired, had worked for most of his life in a blue-collar job. If the spouse of the head of the household was living with the head at the time of the interview, the spouse was included in the sample regardless of age or employment status.

A critical variable of this study was the density of age and social class peers living in the respondents' neighborhoods and the resulting opportunities, or lack of them, for neighborhood social interaction. To permit controls for age and economic peer density, a sample of city blocks at the site of the study, Philadelphia, was taken so that they were spread systematically over the varied neighborhood areas. The 13,754 blocks of the city were arrayed by census tract and ordered geographically in a serpentine manner. A random number was drawn to designate the first block in the sample, and every thirty-fourth block thereafter was selected.

In the second stage of the sampling, a census of households was conducted in the blocks selected. The census had a dual purpose: screening eligible respondents according to the race, age, income, and occupational criteria of the study; and describing the remaining, ineligible, residents of the block. On completion of screening, 230 of the 405 sample blocks were found to contain eligible respondents.[1] They were interviewed at the time they were found. Simultaneously, the social composition of the neighborhood (block) was recorded by gathering information from the respondents' neighbors about their households: relationship of household members to head, age of household members, family income, occupation, and the like. This field work was begun in March, 1965, and was concluded at the end of May, 1965.

The locale of this study and the sample selected from it are in many respects typical of the highly urbanized areas of the United States and of the older poor and modest income blue-collar residents in them. Yet some aspects of Philadelphia and of the lower income levels of its working class distinguish it from other areas. In this final part of our introduction to the study we touch on these similarities and differences in order to provide a perspective for interpreting the results of the analytic chapters which follow.

The economy of Philadelphia is a mixture of elements of

---

[1] Interviews could not be completed in 30 per cent of the households identified as eligible in the screening. This noncompletion level is not unusual in studies of older populations. See, for example, Kutner, Fanshel, Togo, and Langner (1956, p. 269).

permanence and elements of change.[2] The city has been a major
and also a highly diversified manufacturing center since the 1700s
and more importantly has been stable over long periods of time
with respect to the functional structure of its major industries and
the constancy of its business community. Palmer's (1956, pp.
10–11)' data on family heads in 1799 and in 1940 show similar
distributions at both times for manufacturing, trade, transport
and finance, and agriculture. Palmer also documents the existence
today of many of the outstanding businesses that developed manufacturing in the city. The stability and constancy of the Philadelphia
economy appear to be reflected in labor force patterns. Compared
with workers in other cities, Philadelphians are less mobile and
have longer job tenure and longer company attachments. The Philadelphia economy has not, of course, been wholly static, but the basic
industrial pattern has changed slowly.

One such change is the long term decline in some industries
and occupations. In terms of local employment, the city has gained
less in rapidly expanding industries and has lost more in older
manufacturing industries than has the nation as a whole. The
demand for manual as compared with white-collar workers has
been reduced. Since the twenties the metropolitan economy has
been one of persistent depression interrupted by only short periods
of recovery. The cumulative impact on the Philadelphia working
class of the economic conditions sketched here cannot be ascertained.
But since these conditions may bear on the attitudes and activities
of the segment of the working class sampled in this study, we
address ourselves to this question in a limited way in later chapters.
The economic environment of the low and moderately low income
working class people who are our subjects has not been and is not
now a privileged one. If anything, our respondents have lived and
worked under relatively harsh economic conditions. We cannot
say that they are the deprived who have subsisted in the midst of
working class prosperity. To the extent that our respondents have
been aware of the wider economic climate of their city over their
adult years, they probably have perceived stringent economic conditions more than economic comfort among other working people.

[2] The material on the economic background of Philadelphia draws
heavily on Palmer's (1956) study of the Philadelphia working class.

With this background in mind, we devote the remainder of this chapter to a brief profile of our respondents. Some of these data will be reintroduced and dealt with analytically in later chapters.

Age and Income. By the sampling criteria mentioned earlier, we arrived at a study population of 1,596 persons. In the age range of interest, from forty-five to seventy-nine, females naturally are more numerous than males. Thus we have in the sample 908 females (57 per cent of the total) and 688 males (43 per cent of the total). In addition to an imbalanced sex ratio, the distribution of our respondents by age is skewed toward the older years, doubtless because of the study requirement to sample only very low income segments of the working class. Those fifty-four or less make up 29 per cent of the sample, while another 29 per cent is composed of people between fifty-five and sixty-four but 42 per cent of the sample consists of the aged, people between sixty-five and seventy-nine.

What proportion of a sample with an age distribution such as this should we expect to be poor? If the absence of Negroes from the study population leads us to assume that the level of poverty is relatively modest, then the income ceiling imposed on eligibility for inclusion in the sample and the well-known correlation between old age and poverty appear to counterbalance sufficiently the influence of the racial composition. We expect and we do find a sizable proportion of our respondents to be in the poverty category. About 35 per cent, or 565 persons, are poor. Almost all of these belong to households where the income from all sources is less than $3,000 per year. For many, the figure is considerably less. We have also classified as poor twenty-three individuals whose family incomes slightly exceed $3,000 per year—these people have particularly large families. The yearly family incomes of the 65 per cent of our respondents whom we term solvent range between $3,000 and $7,500.

By now we know what to expect of the relation between age and income level: They are inversely related. Among the segment of the white working class in Philadelphia which we sampled, only about 15 per cent of those between forty-five and fifty-four are poor. The proportion in poverty rises in the fifty-five to sixty-four category, where slightly over a quarter of the respondents are poor.

But in the oldest age category, those between sixty-five and seventy-nine, the proportion of poor is double what it is among those just under sixty-five. Over half, 55 per cent, of the aged are poor. This distribution conforms in general to what we know about the relationship of poverty to age among whites in the urban working class throughout the country. However, it also suggests that in the analysis in the following chapters, it will be necessary to hold age level constant in any assessment of the role of poverty or solvency.

The identification of those in the income category we term poverty leaves much unsaid about what the poor are like and the extent to which they differ from the solvent. Income is presumably only one factor, albeit putatively a defining or determining one, in a complex consisting of the attitudes, values, life styles, and social relationships which we have come to associate with poverty and which we have linked to the poverty syndrome ever since Booth (1892) and others began to study the urban poor in Western industrialized societies. In later chapters we spell out in detail the social and cultural connotations of the term *poverty* as it applies to our sample, but at this point we, at the least, would like to know whether our gross distinction between income categories in this working class sample corresponds to feelings or beliefs on the part of our respondents that they are in some sense deprived. If it does, then we can be reassured somewhat of the meaningfulness of the poverty-solvency distinction.

Of the several questions we asked to determine attitudes toward deprivation, the responses to two should suffice here. We asked every person in the sample whether he considered his present income enough to meet living expenses, and found that a considerably higher proportion of the poor (two-thirds) than of the solvent (40 per cent) think their income is insufficient. Again, we asked all but the wives in the sample to rate their ability to provide for their families on a ten-point scale labeled "very poor" at one extreme and "very good" at the other. Dichotomizing the responses at the midpoint of the scale, which also divides the distribution of respondents equally, we obtain a pattern of answers almost identical to the one we observed for the preceding question. A considerably higher proportion of the poverty-stricken (slightly more than two-thirds)' than of the solvent (slightly more than one-third) think their ability to provide for their families is "poor." Thus, to a great extent, those in the sample who are deprived in terms of an objective income standard realize that they are and are willing to admit it. Our analytic distinction between poverty and solvency appears to be an authentic, though gross, correlate of relative amounts of perceived deprivation of those classified poor and solvent.

The sheer fact of low income may not, of course, account for the feelings of deprivation experienced by the respondents. For people over sixty-five it is necessary to assess the independent contribution of retirement to feelings of economic inadequacy. The differences between the poor and the solvent may reflect feelings which have less to do with poverty than with the process of aging and which also may be a function of the different age distributions found among our poor and solvent respondents. Ascertaining what differences in feelings of deprivation still remain between the poor and the solvent when they are grouped into relatively homogeneous age categories should provide an understanding of the sources of perceived deprivation among these older working class people.

Comparing the proportions of poor and solvent people at each age level who think their present income is not enough to meet current living expenses, we see that the income level of our respondents is more strongly associated than their age level with how they feel about their economic position. In addition, a slight decline occurs with increasing age in the proportion of both poor and solvent people who think their income is insufficient. Among the oldest respondents, about 64 per cent of the poor and 39 per cent of the solvent think their income is insufficient. For those between fifty-five, and sixty-four, the figures are 75 and 36 per cent, respectively. And among those fifty-four or less, about 72 per cent of the poor and 46 per cent of the solvent say they do not have enough income. Thus, old age apparently fails to markedly upset the relationship observed above between income level and feelings of sufficiency or insufficiency of income, and whatever small effects age itself may have run in the opposite direction from those we might have supposed.

Before commenting on the possible meaning of this pattern, let us examine how heads of households in the sample, when controlled for age, rate their ability to provide for themselves and their families. Table 1 reveals quite a different kind of reaction to this question on their part. Although the differences between the poor and the solvent remain at all ages—a much smaller proportion of poor people than of solvent people think their ability as providers is "good"—the older people are more pessimistic than the younger. Furthermore, the aged poor are only 9 per cent more pessimistic than the middle-aged poor in this respect, but the solvent aged are 30 per cent more likely than the solvent middle aged to rate their ability as "poor." These findings are the opposite of those we found concerning feelings about sufficiency of income. Moreover, the solvent working class people in this sample exhibit the greater degree of difference between middle and old age in this respect.

This brief excursion into the meaning of deprivation to working class people above and below the poverty line and into the relation of this meaning to age seems to support the following conclusions. The differences in feelings of deprivation between the poor and the solvent are neither a function of age in itself nor an artifact of the age distribution of the poor and the solvent sample members. The overriding influence of income level on feelings of deprivation is nowhere reversed by age, and the appreciably greater pessimism of the poor about their economic circumstances is never reduced to a level low enough to resemble that of the solvent. However, the difference between the poor and the solvent who think their ability to provide is "poor" is half as great among the aged as among those fifty-four or less. This difference occurs because older solvent people are much less optimistic than younger ones, while the older poor differ but little from the younger poor. In addition, for poor and solvent members of the sample alike, the older people feel more optimistic about the current adequacy of their income than do the younger, while the younger feel better able to provide for themselves and their families. Thus, although a very large differential still exists in the proportions of the poor and the solvent who feel this way, there is nevertheless some tendency for all older people to adjust their expenditures and expectations to the lower income levels of the retirement years and at the same time to worry more than the younger people about their ability to care for their families and themselves in general and perhaps in the future. The

Table 1

Felt Ability of Heads of Households to Provide by Age and Income Level

(in percentages)

Ability to Provide	Age					
	65 or More		55 to 64		54 or Less	
	Poor (N = 297)	Solvent (N = 234)	Poor (N = 84)	Solvent (N = 212)	Poor (N = 47)	Solvent (N = 192)
Good	29.3	49.6	38.1	62.3	38.3	79.7
Poor	70.7	50.4	61.9	37.7	61.7	20.3
Total	100.0	100.0	100.0	100.0	100.0	100.0

difference between the older and the younger sample members in the latter respect is, as we have noted, fairly large for the solvent. Between 61 to 72 per cent of the poor at any age know their ability to provide is precarious, but the majority of the solvent perhaps come to realize this only when retirement restricts their earning power.

Social Mobility and Stability. In the very broadest sense the sample is occupationally stable when compared with the parental generation. Our respondents are, for the most part, working class children of working class parents. Approximately 80 per cent of the fathers of the respondents had been employed throughout their lives primarily as blue-collar workers. But even here, in a population which in monetary terms is located at the bottom of the working class, 15 per cent of the respondents have been downwardly mobile over one generation from the upper levels of the middle class. Their fathers were professionals or managers or had kindred occupations. And thus no matter what the children's occupational position within the working class, they have experienced a relatively steep descent. Only about 5 per cent of our working class sample has descended over one generation from an adjacent white-collar level, represented by clerical, sales, and kindred occupations of their fathers.

The occupations of the blue-collar fathers of our respondents reveal a substantial degree of diversity. About 28 per cent of our sample stem from skilled and about 22 per cent from semiskilled occupational levels. Much smaller proportions of the respondents had fathers in service and unskilled occupations. Only 10 per cent of the fathers of the respondents were farmers. We are dealing here with a working class whose agrarian origins are buried in the distant past.

There is another way in which to look at the occupational mobility of the breadwinners in our sample. During their working lives some of our respondents might have changed jobs and in doing so might have altered their occupational level within the working class. We have data for 1935 to 1965 on the occupational histories of the breadwinners in our sample. To measure their career mobility we grouped the various jobs they held into the same categories as those just discussed in terms of fathers' occupation, scored them, performed a regression analysis, and used slope scores to measure the direction of career mobility. Neither the degree of occupational change nor the precise occupational category from which and to which career mobility occurred is of chief interest here. Rather, we wish simply to know the amount of stability and, where there was change, its direction.

Almost two-thirds, about 62 per cent, of these working class breadwinners have been stable with regard to occupational level during this long period. About 20 per cent of them have been upwardly mobile within the working class by this measure; approximately 18 per cent have been downwardly mobile. The thesis that a considerable amount of social stability is characteristic of this segment of the working class is thus reinforced by these career mobility data.

We can gain additional insight by examining our respondents' perceptions of their own career mobility or stability—what are their general conceptions of their movement in terms of broad socioeconomic levels? We asked a series of questions of all the members of the sample concerning their class self-identification: whether they thought they always were in the class with which they currently identify; whether they thought they had moved from one class to another; and if so, when this happened and which classes were the ones from which and into which they moved. Here the data are emphatically clear. These working class people, who, as we have just seen, are largely immobile with respect to occupational level during their careers, are also subjectively immobile. Fully 81 per cent report no interclass movement during their lives. In addition, our respondents' sense of social immobility is fairly constant whether they are aged or middle aged, poor or solvent. Within each of the three age categories, between 78 and 86 per cent of poor and of solvent people think of themselves as immobile. Only among the youngest group of the poor, those under fifty-four, is there an appreciable departure from this range. Sixty-six per cent think of themselves as immobile—still a very substantial proportion.

In Table 2 the 293 individuals (19 per cent of the sample) who believe they have changed social classes are arrayed by age and, within each age category, by income level. They are classified by perceived upward and downward mobility. The few individuals who think they have moved up first and then down or down and then up are noted as mixed types. Table 2 shows that the perceived direction of social mobility is related both to income level and to age. First, in each age category an appreciably larger proportion of poor than of solvent people think they have moved downward in the class hierarchy, and an appreciably larger proportion of solvent than of poor people think they have moved upward. Poverty and solvency, then, are related in an expectable way to whether people think they have come up or down in the world. Second, the difference between poor and solvent, within each age category, decreases markedly from middle age through the retirement decade and into old age. The aged poor, in greater proportion than the younger poor, think they have been upwardly mobile; and proportionally fewer of the aged solvent than of the younger solvent people think they have been upwardly mobile.

To ascertain the reasons for this seeming paradox in perceived mobility, we asked those who thought they had moved from one class to another in which year their mobility occurred. These dates were converted into the respondents' ages at the time of mobility. Table 3 reveals that no matter what their present age, proportionally more solvent people than poor people think they have been mobile when they were relatively young. Forty-five years seems to be the dividing line: A larger percentage of the solvent than of the poor think they were mobile at a younger age than forty-five, and a larger percentage of the poor than of the solvent think they were mobile after they passed their forty-fifth birthday. Since the solvent assign their mobility to the days of their early maturity and since, relative to the views of the poor, much of it has been perceived as upward mobility, when they are asked at older ages to state the direction in which they have moved, understandably a larger percentage of the older than of the younger solvent people think they have come down in the world. For the realities of working class life are such that, having made some initial socioeconomic gain (most probably an occupational advance), the working man reaches a plateau he can rarely exceed. And this usually happens fairly early in his career.

The poor, on the other hand, assign their mobility to later middle age in greater proportions than do the solvent. And in

Table 2

PERCEIVED DIRECTION OF INTERCLASS MOVEMENT BY AGE AND INCOME LEVEL

(in percentages)[a]

Perceived Direction	Age					
	65 or More		55 to 64		54 or Less	
	Poor (N = 73)	Solvent (N = 51)	Poor (N = 27)	Solvent (N = 62)	Poor (N = 24)	Solvent (N = 56)
Up	28.7	49.0	18.5	43.5	16.7	66.1
Down	63.0	49.0	74.1	41.9	83.3	25.0
Mixed	8.2	2.0	7.4	14.6	0.0	8.9
Total	100.0	100.0	100.0	100.0	100.0	100.0

[a] Percentages may not add to 100 because of rounding.

Table 3

Age at Which Perceived Interclass Movement Occurred By Current Age and Income Level

(in percentages)[a]

Age at Interclass Movement[b]	Age					
	65 or More		55 to 64		54 or Less	
	Poor (N = 73)	Solvent (N = 50)	Poor (N = 27)	Solvent (N = 62)	Poor (N = 23)	Solvent (N = 55)
65 or more	20.5	26.0	—	—	—	—
45 to 64	39.7	24.0	70.4	40.3	39.1	12.7
25 to 44	27.4	30.0	22.2	40.3	52.2	52.7
24 or less	12.3	20.0	7.4	19.4	8.7	34.5
Total	100.0	100.0	100.00	100.0	100.0	100.0

[a] Percentages may not add to 100 because of rounding.
[b] Excludes three no answers.

comparison to the solvent, many of the poor think they have moved downward. If we are to understand why older poor people think they have come down in the world in smaller proportions than younger poor people, we must assume that there is something about the years in which the younger poor experienced their mobility which leads them to take a different frame of reference from that of the poor who are past retirement age. The mobility of these younger poor people, which they claim took place after they were forty-five, occurred from 1945 to 1965. Much of the mobility which the retirement-age poor people say occurred after they were forty-five could have taken place as early as 1930. If the older poor have the depression years as a benchmark for evaluating the direction of their own mobility, a larger proportion of them than of the younger poor may well think that they have moved up and a smaller proportion that they have moved down. Hence Table 2 most probably represents the differential impact, on poor and solvent working class people who think they have been socially mobile, of both age-specific career trends and exposure to particular historical events.

Along with intergenerational and career mobility, another indicator of the degree of social stability of this working class sample is geographical movement. We noted earlier that only a small percentage of these Philadelphia working class people had fathers who were farmers. And indeed, 71 per cent of the sample grew up in a big city, 17 per cent grew up in a small town, and only 3 per cent spent their childhood in the suburb of a big city. Of the remainder, who were raised outside urban areas, 7 per cent grew up on a farm and 2 per cent in a rural area but not on a farm. In addition to experiencing an urban upbringing, most members (90 per cent) of the sample are native Philadelphians or long term residents of the city.

These residents do not move from one address to another within Philadelphia with much frequency. About 39 per cent of the sample have resided at their current address for over twenty years, in sharp contrast to the amount of residential mobility experienced by the population of the city as a whole. Only about 17 per cent of the total population of Philadelphia moved into the housing unit they occupied in 1960 prior to 1940 according to the U.S. Bureau

of the Census (1962, p. 417). And although 59 per cent of the
population of Philadelphia have resided in the same unit for more
than five years, about 83 per cent of the sample have lived at the
same address for more than five years. The residential stability of
the members of the sample can be explained in large part by the
fact that most of them are homeowners. Only 16 per cent of the
families in our sample live in apartments. The remainder are
resident-owners of row houses or detached dwellings. Philadelphians
in general have one of the highest home-ownership rates of the
residents of any city in the country. However, it is not surprising in
view of the nature of the housing accommodations in the city that
a low income, working class sample should consist chiefly of homeowners. A large proportion of Philadelphia houses are old row
houses, a situation which encourages the taking of mortgages rather
than leases. And although there are notable exceptions, much of
the recent residential construction in the city has been of high-rise
apartment buildings with rentals scaled to the middle class and
luxury market.

Additional Characteristics. Several characteristics of the
respondents in addition to those already discussed are relevant to
our study. The sample is disproportionately composed of immigrants
and foreign stock. Slightly more than 29 per cent of the respondents
were born outside the United States. An additional 36 per cent
had at least one foreign born parent. According to the U.S. Bureau
of the Census (1962, p. 21), Philadelphia in 1960 contained less
than a third the proportion of immigrants, approximately 9 per
cent, than is found among our respondents. And the sample contains more than twice the proportion of foreign stock found in the
city as a whole. However, the proportional distribution by country
of origin of the immigrants in the sample approximates that of
Philadelphia immigrants in general, with Italy, Russia, and Ireland
the three most popular native lands. Hence, by restricting our
sample to white working class people of low income and old age,
we have overrepresented the foreign born and first generation but
have not distorted appreciably the distribution of immigrants by
country of origin.

Philadelphia has a large Roman Catholic population, and
among working class people in general, Catholics are likely to be

overrepresented in comparison with Protestants. This geographic concentration of Catholics combined with the well-known association between low socioeconomic standing and being born a Catholic, which in Philadelphia is also partly a function of a history of immigration from Italy and Ireland, produce a sample over 55 per cent of which is Catholic. About 29 per cent of the respondents are Protestant, and almost 13 per cent are Jewish.

All the above characteristics, plus age and income level, ensure that the number of years of schooling of our respondents will be relatively few. Only twenty-seven of the respondents, slightly more than 1 per cent, attended college at all, about 12 per cent completed high school, and the remaining 86 per cent had less than a complete high school education—with 36 per cent not completing elementary school. Compared with all Philadelphians twenty-five or over, the members of the sample have less education. For example, over 10 per cent of the city population attended some college, while only 26 per cent failed to complete elementary school.

In addition to having completed fewer years of school than the rest of the population, a relatively smaller proportion of our respondents are employed. This, of course, is not a function of an exceptional rate of unemployment, for in this sample 4.4 per cent of the respondents are not retired but are not working and are seeking employment. About 35 per cent of the sample are not working and are not looking for jobs—these are mainly women. Another 31 per cent are retired. And a final 30 per cent are actively participating in the labor force—25 per cent full time and 5 per cent part time.

The 530 married couples in the study make up two-thirds of the sample. Twenty-two per cent of our respondents, or 351 persons, are widowed. About 6 per cent, ninety-nine people, have never been married; and almost 4 per cent have been divorced and are not presently married or are separated from spouses. A small number of individuals, twenty-four (1½ per cent of the sample), have domestic arrangements not encompassed by the standard categories of nuptuality. All these marital arrangements are found in a total of 1,026 households. The conjugal pair and the nuclear family are the modal family types in this sample, 28 and 19 per cent, respectively, of all households. But there is almost as large a proportion of solitary females, 18 per cent, as of nuclear families. Nuclear families without a male head are also fairly numerous, making up 9 per cent of the households. And solitary males account for another 8 per cent. The proportion of conjugal pairs and nuclear families, either intact or truncated, who live with other relatives is 13 per cent of the total number of households. If we assume that conjugal pairs or nuclear families living without other kin in their households are the conventional domiciliary forms, then 47 per cent of the households are so constituted, and the remaining majority of households have unconventional arrangements.

In this chapter we have seen that our sampling strictures have resulted in a study population made up of the stable, lower segment of the white working class in the older age range. We place special weight on the social immobility of our respondents as represented by their relatively low degree of intergenerational and career vertical mobility and by their long tenure of residence in Philadelphia and in their present domiciles. The social and physical immobility we have found leads us to suspect that favorable conditions exist for the integration of these working class people into local friendship and kinship relations.

Social Class Context of Friendship

Of friends made with a view to pleasure, also, few are enough, as a little seasoning in food is enough.

And whatever existence means for each class of men, whatever it is for whose sake they value life, in that they wish to occupy themselves with their friends . . . for from each other they take the mould of the characteristics they approve.

ARISTOTLE
Nicomachean Ethics

23

The concept of social isolation has often been formulated in a holistic manner, as is reflected in the use of composite indexes to assess the extent or lack of social activity. These indexes usually refer to many of the forms of social contact which can occur among a diversity of people who may stand, moreover, in a multitude of possible social relationships—kin, friends, neighbors, casual acquaintances, coworkers, supervisors, clients, customers, and the like. Hence, in studies of social stratification as well as of aging, measures abound which purport to indicate the nature of social worlds, life spaces, social fields, and similar conceptions. Our instruments are frequently inventories, and the theoretical entities they represent are frequently global.

The kinds of questions which have been asked about social isolation are responsible, chiefly, for this holistic emphasis. Recent investigation, undeniably based on long traditions of social thought and research, has addressed itself to questions of wide substantive scope or broad theoretical nature—though seldom both in the same work. Are the aged more isolated than younger people? Is what we term social isolation part of an intrinsic developmental tendency which culminates with death? Is there more social isolation in the working than in the middle class? Are putative class differences in isolation a function of the organization of work and of attitudes toward work or of the differential impact of the business cycle on manual and nonmanual workers or of sheer level of income? Are differences in amounts of social isolation attributable to age or class? Or are the dislocations in the social system so broad that a lack of the means to reach desired or desirable goals renders these goals unattainable in fact and promotes withdrawal from social interaction?

Questions such as these do not necessarily contain injunctions to consider the separate forms which isolation may take or to search for finer differences among subcategories of age and class. As a consequence, heavy emphasis has been placed on a varied array of relatively gross independent variables, and comparatively little attention has been paid to the dependent variables. Although

24

there are notable exceptions to this typical mode of studying social isolation—some of them have been cited in the preceding chapter and some will be referred to shortly—the separable dimensions of social isolation receive attention almost coincidentally—for example, when one or more of them become institutionalized as the object of inquiry of a particular area of the social sciences. Family sociology, in its long-standing concern with the isolation of the nuclear family and the viability of the extended kin network, is the most prominent case in point.

At the very least, it seems necessary to differentiate two structural aspects of social isolation—isolation from friends and isolation from kin—and to treat each separately. Individual choice plays a greater role in the formation of friendships than in kinship interaction. And there is no counterpart in friendship relations to the ascriptive obligations governing family relationships. The kinds of behavior prescribed and permitted among friends and among kin may overlap, but there remain large areas of social interaction and feelings not common to the two spheres of relations. When friendships do overreach in scope and intimacy their conventionally defined bounds, the especially close friend (usually also one of long duration) becomes known as aunt or uncle. There are ample grounds, therefore, for assuming that the dynamics of social participation and social isolation differ where kinship and friendship are concerned.

This chapter, then, is about patterns of friendship and isolation from friends among the working class of Philadelphia. It examines the way small environments within the city influence informal social relations and contribute to the lack of them. In particular, it is about the impact on the friendship patterns of poor and solvent working class people, in middle and advanced age, of certain urban neighborhood conditions connected with social class: level of wealth, occupational composition, and racial mixture. (In the following chapter we consider other neighborhood characteristics: age structure, marital condition, and population size and density.)

Much of what is known about friendships among adults is a result of comparative studies of the working and middle class. In general, these studies present consistent findings (although there is no such consensus in interpreting them). They indicate that lack of friends or infrequent contact with friends is inversely correlated with position in the socioeconomic hierarchy.[1] Indeed, the epigraph for much recent research on the relative amount of lower or working class contact with friends may well be the often quoted words of Knupfer's (1947)' classic synthesis "Even in face-to-face contacts [lower status] people are more limited. Informal·social activities, such as visiting friends, are more infrequent among them. . . . What friendship contacts there are among [lower class] people are apt to be confined to a narrower area."

The agreement of comparative studies spanning several generations of research has lent an air of conclusiveness to our conception of working class friendship patterns. In accepting gross interclass comparisons, we tend to think of each class as a whole and to neglect to search for intraclass variability. Instead, research investment has been made in other issues, mainly those concerned with interpreting the observed low level of interaction with friends in the working class. Few investigators have studied the possibility that substantial variation in amount of interaction with friends may exist within the working class itself.

An initial look at our own data seems to confirm some of the existing knowledge about working class friendships. We obtained information about friendships in the following manner. Respondents were asked, "Thinking back over the past seven days, could you tell me which of your friends or neighbors you have visited with or talked to?" If the respondent was working, visits during work were excluded. A visit or a conversation with a friend or neighbor was interpreted broadly. A phone conversation with a friend, for example, was considered a legitimate interaction. The interviewer listed by name all friends thus reported by the respondent. After completing this listing, the interviewer questioned the respondent further concerning the first friend reported and then repeated this question for each friend in turn. By having the respondent name all his friends before telling us anything about

[1] For summaries of this literature, see Hodges (1964, Ch. 6, especially pp. 120–23) and Kahl (1957, Ch. 5, especially pp. 141–47). See also, the interesting synthesis and interpretation of much data on working class primary relationships, including friendship, by Blum (1964).

them, we believe we largely avoided the possibility of certain kinds of value-biased responses. If, for example, we had asked outright, "What are your friends' occupations?", respondents might have reported only those friends with higher occupations in order to impress the interviewer.

In the week preceding the interview, one-third of our sample did not visit with or speak to a friend or neighbor. (This substantial proportion are considered isolates in this study.) About 44 per cent visited or conversed with only one or two friends during this period, and approximately 12 per cent had contact with three friends. Having small numbers of friends seems to be the rule.

Moreover, as others have pointed out, the friends of working class people tend to be their neighbors. Of those Philadelphians who had contact with friends during the preceding week, only about 27 per cent had all their friends living outside the immediate neighborhood, that is, more distant than the respondent's block.

In addition, frequent contacts (three times a week or more) with friends were reported by slightly less than half of those who saw a friend during the past week. Since we counted quite casual contacts, some of this interaction probably was more or less perfunctory. Therefore, intensive contact with friends does not seem to characterize more than about a third of the entire sample.

In Chapter One we raised the question of the possible relation of age and economic standing to social isolation. Either poverty or old age or perhaps both jointly may affect isolation from friends within the working class. Insofar as sheer contact with friends is concerned, the evidence does not bear out this supposition. The poor and the solvent have among them the same proportion of isolates: 35 and 36 per cent, respectively. The proportion of isolates among those of different ages does not differ appreciably: 29 per cent among those fifty-four or younger, 36 per cent among those between fifty-five and sixty-four, and 37 per cent among those sixty-five or older. Considering the impact of poverty on friendship separately for each age level, we can detect no appreciable difference in the amount of isolation. Among those over sixty-five 35 per cent of the poor and 40 per cent of the solvent are isolated. For those between fifty-five and sixty-four, the respective percentages are 39 and 34. And among respondents fifty-four or less, 32 per cent of the poor and 28 per cent of the solvent are isolated. Neither age nor income level, separately or jointly, sufficiently distinguished those who are and those who are not isolated from friends.

Before exploring further the nature of isolation from friends, we should point out the specific connection of friendship relations with some other social activities. Lack of interaction with friends does not necessarily entail abstention from other forms of social intercourse. We asked our respondents, "During the last seven days, how many times did you go out to a store, a religious service, a meeting of any kind, a park or zoo, any other place? Did you go out at all?" Only small differences become evident between the isolates and nonisolates. A slightly larger percentage of those isolated from friends went nowhere at all in the past week. And proportionately more isolates than those with friends went out at least once to only one place, while a larger percentage of those with friends went to several places. But the differences are of an order of magnitude of only 7 to 12 per cent. In addition, when they went to a store, a park, a meeting, and the like, similar proportions (61 per cent of the isolates and 51 per cent of those with friends) did so by themselves. Thus, those isolated from friends are not also recluses: Only very small proportions of isolates (and nonisolates) failed to engage in any of the activities about which they were questioned. And even when 61 per cent of those isolated from friends report that they went out alone to a store, a meeting, and the like, we cannot exclude the possibility that the casual human contact represented by such social activities may have been as meaningful or as satisfying to them as relationships with friends were to those we do not consider isolated. Although in this study we are not in a position to investigate in detail the meaning of these casual social activities to our respondents, we would be mistaken if we ruled out the likelihood that in some affective sense they represented alternatives to friendships. Thus, isolation from primary social relationships does not also imply isolation from secondary social activities. And although there is no evidence that isolation from primary activities leads in a compensatory way to more frequent participation in secondary relationships, neither is there any reason to suppose that it is an indication of total social withdrawal.

This brief digression into areas of social life not concerned with friends was necessary to show that the analysis of friendship patterns and particularly of isolation from friends should not be conceived as an undifferentiated part of the more general question of the level of over-all social activity which obtains within the working class. The particular pattern of relationships termed *friendship* and the conditions under which poverty and age may contribute to a lack of friends among working class people are more properly analyzed within the framework of the social conditions which are distinctively the setting of working class life and which bear closely upon friendship patterns per se and not within the framework of friendship patterns as simply another facet of social activity in general. Moreover, when commentators such as Blum (1964) point out that much work on interclass comparisons of friendship and other primary relations has assumed that low status is a precondition for withdrawal from primary involvement, they may indeed tacitly recognize differential bases for primary and secondary involvement. But also the point states in the form of a necessary relationship what has heretofore been observed as a correlation and then makes the observed empirical regularity a fundamental assumption. Beyond this, however, the implied point of view imputes to virtually any low ranking position extreme potency in influencing rates of interaction with kin, with friends, and in other primary affiliations. Whether or not low status is a precondition for withdrawal, such a statement fails to specify what in the social system of the working class is crucial in accounting for withdrawal. Additionally, we are left without a clue about whether there is uniformity or variability in the extent to which withdrawal applies to the segments and subgroupings of that diverse population termed the working class. Therefore, it is appropriate now to examine the social setting of working class life to find the conditions which may contribute to lack of and to participation in friendship relations.

THE NEIGHBORHOOD

A recurrent observation in a wide variety of studies is the importance of the neighborhood to its working class residents. In Whyte's (1943) classic study of a Boston Italian immigrant slum, for example, the neighborhood emerges as an environment encompassing most of the nonwork social interaction of many of its inhabitants. Emotional ties to the area usually remain strong throughout life, even if the slum-dweller moves to another part of the city. Of course, not all working class people identify closely with the neighborhood. Whyte calls attention to the "college boys" for whom neighborhood ties and involvement have been subordinated to aspirations for upward social mobility. Approximately twenty years after Whyte's, a study by Gans (1962, especially Ch. 5 and pp. 89–97) of a Boston working class district, also primarily Italian-American, qualified, but did not replace, Whyte's conception of the neighborhood as the central arena of social life. Centrality of the neighborhood in the lives of the working class also is noted in English studies. Hoggart (1957, especially pp. 51–61) sensitively describes the all-embracing character of working class neighborhood life of several generations ago. Young and Willmott (1957, pp. 104–18) stress the current importance of residence and the way life is played out in limited physical space in the East London borough of Bethnal Green. In addition, Bell (1957), Bell and Boat (1957), Smith, Form, and Stone (1954), and Rosow (1967) note the heavy dependence of the working class upon the neighborhood as a source of friends—a finding which conforms to our own. Also, Kriesberg and Bellin (1965, pp. 37–61) discuss the isolation from the surrounding neighborhoods of the poor residents of four public housing projects.

There is, then, substantial indication of the past and present salience of the local area for the urban working class. However, this local area is very circumscribed. Gans (1962, pp. 11, 105) stresses the interest of people in and their attachment to *"their* street." The locus of the social world of the subjects of Whyte's (1943) study is "Norton Street," and mainly the corner at that. Hoggart (1957) notes that an area only a block away seems unfamiliar to urban workers. The friendliness displayed to people living close by in the same street is noticed by Young and Willmott (1957), who characterize a street as "a sort of 'village' of 100 to 200 people" (p. 109). They fix the area in which residents feel a sense of community as being no wider than some adjacent streets. In 1886 Charles Booth (1892, p. 27), in discussing residential moves in Bethnal Green, remarked that although a large proportion of those with children in school moved during the year, "on the whole

. . . the people usually do not go far, and often cling from generation to generation to one vicinity, almost as if the set of streets
which lie there were an isolated country village."

Although many studies of the working class which include
neighborhood variables are based on areas larger than a block,
usually a census tract, and although many of them deal with forms
of social interaction other than friendship, they may indicate which
aspects of neighborhoods significantly influence friendship patterns
and isolation from friends in areas smaller than the tract. Thus,
in an analysis of interaction with kin, Bell and Boat (1957) point
out that in neighborhoods of low economic status slightly greater
proportions of adult males have never had contact with relatives
(or see them only about once a year) than is the case in higher
status areas.

Concerning friendship, residents of low economic areas,
more than those who live in middle class areas, rely on their immediate neighborhood for friends according to Smith, Form, and
Stone (1954). A larger percentage of white-collar than of blue-
collar persons report that they seldom see their neighbors in predominantly blue-collar census tracts, but the reverse is the case in
predominantly white-collar tracts, Bell (1961) reports. The extent
to which friendships form after old people lose spouses depends upon
the prevalence of others with similar role losses in the community,
Blau (1961) suggests. But this was true for the middle and not
for the lower classes in her sample. In one of the few studies to
employ very small local environments, Rosow (1967) defines an
apartment house as a neighborhood context. In a large sample of
Cleveland, Ohio, apartment houses, he found that as the density of
age peers in the building increased, older working class residents increasingly tended to select age peers as friends. A parallel pattern
obtained for middle class residents, but not to such a pronounced
degree.

Concerning group membership, in two Florida communities
of unequal socioeconomic status Webber (1954) found that in the
wealthy community retirees seventy and above had more voluntary
association memberships than did those in their fifties and sixties. In
a less wealthy community the younger retirees had more memberships. In a study of four San Francisco census tracts of varying

occupational, educational, and income compositions Bell and Force (1956) found a similar association between neighborhood type and group membership.

Finally, a few characterizations of neighborhoods by the presence of kin have been made in an attempt to relate the neighborhood kinship context to local friendships formed by the residents. The proximity of kin and the length of time kin have lived nearby may be important factors, although not the only ones which encourage local friendships. Young and Willmott (1957, p. 116) state, "Either length of residence or localized kinship does something to create a network of local attachment, but when they are combined, as they are in Bethnal Green, they constitute a much more powerful force than when one exists without the other." And McGough (1964, p. 39) found a high correlation between the presence of relatives and of many close friends in selected census tracts in West Philadelphia.

We have, then, ample evidence that the immediate neighborhood is a relevant context of working class social life, including working class friendships. (It may not, of course, be the only important element affecting friendship formation; Lazarsfeld and Merton (1954) suggest value homophily as another.) More precisely, the social composition of the neighborhood, in particular the economic, occupational, and age characteristics of its inhabitants, is consequential for friendships or the absence of friendships among working class people. And apparently the economic composition of the neighborhood also influences their frequency of contact with kin and participation in voluntary associations. (We reserve discussion of kin for a later chapter.)

Most of the findings on local social participation discussed so far can be subsumed under a general statement: The more the neighborhood is populated by others with similar social characteristics, the more an individual is led to associate with others. Blau's and Rosow's data clearly imply that these others also live in the neighborhood. But the rest of the studies imply at least some amount of spillover into areas beyond the neighborhood. Also, the converse of the statement appears to apply to friendship: The more the neighborhood is populated by others with dissimilar social characteristics, the more individuals are led to withdraw from association with others in the neighborhood. But the extent to which they may seek elsewhere for friends is not clear in all cases—the presumption is that by and large working class people do not seek elsewhere to a great extent and that middle class people do.

From these and comparable findings, the neighborhood can be seen as the social context of friendship interactions. It limits the likelihood of given individuals' making friends within its confines according to whether it provides an environment rich in status-similars. We are not prepared to argue at this point whether the friendships made within the neighborhood are in a few or in many cases based upon status homophily. Nor need we now explore the various mechanisms other than status homophily which alleviate conflict within the role set and thereby promote interaction among friends. Here it is necessary to note only when occupational, economic, marital, and age peers, as well as others we consider later in this chapter and the subsequent one, are present in the neighborhood in some as yet undetermined amount, the likelihood of isolation from friends is reduced, and the probability of friendly interaction with neighbors is increased for individuals whose statuses correspond with the local norm. Moreover, when individual residents of the same neighborhood differ from each other in the status attributes with which we are concerned, in all likelihood they display different patterns of affiliation with friends.

We have located in the neighborhood, then, the sociologically critical locus for the study of working class friendships. And we have imputed to the neighborhood social structure some of the functions of a social context. It has been customary to view social contexts as constraining the performance of certain tasks, the maintenance of certain behavior patterns, or the espousal of certain ideas. As Merton (1957, p. 53) points out, the concept of social context comes to us in part through an anthropological tradition which emphasized the manner in which social structures limited possibilities of various sorts. However, in our view neighborhood social structure is a contextual entity which may serve equally as a limiting or as an enabling environment for friendship formation and maintenance. Or, to put it another way, the contextual function of neighborhood social structure governs the rate at which a given pattern of social relations occurs. Isolation from friends simply represents a rate of zero. Whether a given structural context is enabling or limiting depends on the direction of the rate of friendship relations—toward zero or toward a high rate. However, the determination of the direction of the rate of friendship does not rest exclusively on the contextual variable. It depends also upon the interaction of a particular structural context with a given attribute of the individual embedded in that context. The context which enables one person to form numerous friendships limits another person with different characteristics to few friends or to none. Thus the utility of the concept of structural context does not necessarily lie wholly in the identification of certain features of the social environment. Rather, its worth in analysis is that it forces us to consider various forms of relationship between the structure of the social environment and the individuals whose social activities take place within that environment.

Another implication of the foregoing studies concerns the different structural contexts which may have identical effects on friendship relations and on other forms of primary social participation. There may be a range of alternative structural contexts each of which restricts or increases the rate of interaction with friends in precisely the same way or to precisely the same extent. If this were found to be the case, it would raise the question of whether there is a degree of ambiguity in the social structure such that any number of contextual forms can serve the same function vis-à-vis friendship relations. Before we accept such a formulation and are tempted to identify areas of indifference in the society, we should consider again that the relationship between individual and contextual characteristics, and not solely the impress of the structural context, governs the rate of friendship interaction. In principle, when we find an array of structural contexts (age contexts, occupational contexts, racial contexts, and the like) which appear to be diverse in character and yet which have identical effects in patterning friendship relations, we may have an artifact of our excessively narrow conception of the nature of the contexts involved. Once we have reconsidered a diversity of contexts for the purpose of finding whether their prima facie dissimilarity has prevented us from seeing that they all stand in a similar relationship to some particular characteristic of the individuals whose friendship rates they are affecting, a number of structural contexts may no longer seem diverse insofar as their relationship to individuals with specific social characteristics is concerned. If we think initially of these contexts as representing an area of indifference, we may neglect to search for the sociological similarity amid substantive diversity.

One further consideration to be derived from studies of working class localism is the notion of the strength of a structural context. For example, a moderately wealthy neighborhood may not contain as many isolated working class residents as does an extremely wealthy neighborhood. Or the contextual effect may not be monotonic but instead may occur at a tipping point when, for example, a rate of isolation remains negligible until a certain level of neighborhood wealth obtains, at which point the isolation rate changes markedly. In such instances the relationship between the attributes of individuals whose friendship rates are being considered and the contextual characteristic involves either a mechanism which operates in a wide range of social settings or one which requires certain specific, measurable conditions for its operation. In both cases, such contextual effects are to be distinguished from those in a situation in which one context is more potent in its effects than another is. When an age context, for example, has little influence on the rate of social isolation from friends while a racial context has much influence, then perhaps the relationships between the individuals involved and the contextual characteristic differ from one instance to the other. In this latter situation, the notion of the strength of a context may not be relevant.

We now can formulate the problem of isolation from friends more adequately. The simplistic notion that poverty and age are correlated directly with isolation from friends is misleading, according to both our own data presented above and, by analogy, to other studies comparing middle and working class friendship patterns. Rather, it is a more complex problem of determining how variable is the degree of isolation within different social structures, now identified as neighborhoods of small area, and how isolation varies within these differing structural contexts for persons with different age and income attributes.

Analysis of isolation from friends, thus conceived, requires that we consider simultaneously several aspects of friendship patterns. We must compare isolates, those with no friends, with two other categories: those who do have friends within the neighborhood and those who do not have friends within the neighborhood but who maintain active friendships beyond its confines. The impact of neighborhood structural contexts on friendship cannot be assessed until it is known whether the result of living in a given social environment is integration into a local network of friends or transfer of the locus of friendship elsewhere or utter isolation.

SOCIOECONOMIC STATUS

We turn now to a consideration of the friendship relations and of the isolation from friends of the members of our white working class sample of middle-aged and older Philadelphians. We first discuss a number of structural contexts which on a priori grounds we would expect to have similar effects on friendship relations. These contexts are components of the socioeconomic rank of the residents of a neighborhood: income, occupation, and race. Monetary, occupational, and racial factors, it is true, do not stand in the same relations to social class. Occupation is most often employed in defining the class membership of individuals; income and wealth have been taken as determinants, consequences, and correlates of class position; and race has been alleged to contribute in a number of ways to differential class placement. But insofar as the neighborhood is concerned, each of these factors provides a basis for invidious distinction in friendship relations, whatever differences may exist among them in their more general roles as factors in social class analysis. What we do expect and see shortly is that these diverse contexts affect friendships and isolation from friends of the poor and of the solvent people of the working class in Philadelphia neighborhoods in similar ways. In addition, we recognize that a common theme is the greater responsiveness of the solvent working class people than of the poor, at a given age level, to the effects of socioeconomic status contexts on friendships.

Economic Context. Poor people in wealthy neighborhoods and solvent people in poor neighborhoods both may lack friends because they reside where the over-all level of wealth differs from their own. We measure the wealth of a neighborhood here by the mean income per annum of its constituent families. The differential impact of neighborhood wealth, thus measured, upon the poor and the solvent is examined separately for working class people of different ages.

Table 4 shows that the increasingly higher economic level of the neighborhood enables increasingly larger proportions of solvent old men to maintain local friendships and limits local friendships to progressively smaller proportions of the poor old men. And the differential in the proportion of poor and solvent with local friendships is maintained even in the wealthiest neighborhoods. But the relationship between isolation and neighborhood wealth, although it does not diverge as strongly as that between local friendship and neighborhood wealth, nevertheless remains complementary to it.

It is not necessary to assume that two mechanisms are involved in order to characterize adequately the increase of isolation among the poor and the decrease of isolation among the solvent old men under identical conditions of neighborhood wealth. Since at this point we seek to interpret the direction of these rates in contexts of increasing wealth, rather than to account for the absolute magnitude of any given percentage, we can arrive at a single formulation which encompasses the divergent rates without attributing to the poor some special characteristic responsible for their isolation in situations where the solvent find it possible to maintain friendships. The patterns of friendship and isolation from friends revealed in different contexts of neighborhood wealth are the effects of what Rosenberg (1962) terms dissonant and consonant contexts. The relationship between an individual characteristic and a characteristic of the surrounding social environment may be similar or dissimilar. Solvent people in low income neighborhoods and poor people in higher income neighborhoods both reside in dissonant economic contexts. Solvent people in wealthy areas, however, reside in a more consonant economic context, as do poor people in poor areas. Dissonant contexts promote more individual isolation and less friendship within the area defined by the contextual variable, and consonant contexts have the opposite effect. The data in Table 4 demonstrate this point.

However, solvent and poor old men do not feel equally the strength of neighborhood contextual dissonance and consonance

Table 4

FRIENDSHIP PATTERNS OF POOR AND SOLVENT MALES, AGE SIXTY-FIVE OR MORE, BY NEIGHBORHOOD ECONOMIC LEVEL
(in percentages)[a]

Friendship Patterns	Poor			Solvent		
	Mean Yearly Family Income of Neighborhood					
	$4,000 or Less (N = 41)	$4,001 to $5,000 (N = 54)	$5,001 or More (N = 57)	$4,000 or Less (N = 22)	$4,001 to $5,000 (N = 77)	$5,001 or More (N = 74)
Isolates	26.8	33.3	40.4	54.5	45.5	29.7
Friends beyond the neighborhood	9.8	18.5	21.1	18.2	26.0	17.6
Friends within the neighborhood	63.4	48.1	38.6	27.3	28.6	52.7
Total	100.0	100.0	100.0	100.0	100.0	100.0

[a] Percentages may not add to 100 because of rounding.

in patterning friendship relations. The solvent are more responsive to the influence of the economic context than are the poor, as far as isolation is concerned. The difference in proportion of isolates between those in consonant and those in dissonant contexts is larger for the solvent than for the poor, as Table 4 indicates. The relative lack of responsiveness of the poor, however, works to their advantage, for the consequences of living in a dissonant context, among income-dissimilars, are not as severe for them as for the solvent men. More of the poor than of the solvent old men can find local friends in economically dissonant neighborhoods. Although a relatively large proportion of the poor old men who live in rich areas have friends beyond the neighborhood (Table 4), proportionately more of them have local friends in rich neighborhoods than do solvent old men living in poor neighborhoods.

What makes the poor respond to income differences in a way that enables them to maintain primary participation in dissonant social settings? We are unable to answer this question in a wholly satisfactory manner at this point because we do not know whether the poor form friendships with wealthier neighbors or with others who are also impoverished. Furthermore, we need to know the extent to which people who are better off financially constitute reference groups with which the poor compare themselves. We can note only that the relative strength of dissonant contexts may be related to the differential implications of primary participation for poor and solvent old men in such settings. When the poor maintain friendships in a neighborhood context of relative wealth, they may gain something of a vicarious reward, while for solvent old men, the maintenance of friendships in neighborhoods of low income level may represent invidious social stigmatization. Such an interpretation of the relative strength, for poor and solvent, of dissonant contexts does not necessarily require that friendships be maintained among income-dissimilars. Vicarious reward for the poor and invidious stigmatization for the solvent may be enhanced all the more if they occur through the medium of income homophilous interaction since common values are realized more readily among status-equals.

The influence of neighborhood income contexts is a class-linked phenomenon and as such is relevant mainly to those who have close structural connection with the socioeconomic ranking of the society. Therefore, when we look at the friendship patterns of women sixty-five or more, we do not expect to find, as we did for old men, that contextual dissonance promotes isolation. Of the major age and sex categories in this sample, old women are the most tenuously class linked. Middle-aged women are more involved than old women in the social class system through their husbands, who are still in the labor force. In view of the irrelevancy of these socioeconomic matters for women in the postretirement years, the sources of their isolation from friends cannot be found in the structural context of neighborhood wealth. Increasingly wealthy neighborhoods neither appreciably increase the isolation of poor old women nor decrease the isolation of solvent old women. Although we are handicapped in our interpretation by the small numbers of solvent old women who live in poor neighborhoods, by and large women are subject to the impact of neighborhood wealth on neighborhood friendships in a radically different way from men. For example, proportionately few of the solvent old women who live in the richest neighborhoods have local friends. A relatively large proportion of these women are isolates in the very environment which for the men is most conducive to reduced isolation.

This relatively high level of isolation probably stems from the existence of surviving husbands to whom they, in contrast to unmarried women, can turn for companionship. And the same reasoning applies to the poor old women, we would expect, who live in wealthy neighborhoods. Some support for this interpretation exists in our data, which, although based on small numbers of cases, are suggestive nevertheless. In wealthy neighborhoods, half the married women, whether poor or solvent, have no friends at all. But a quarter of the poor unmarried and a third of the solvent unmarried women are isolated. As far as local friendships are concerned, about a third of the married women, whether poor or solvent, have friends in the neighborhood, as do a third of the unmarried solvent women. But in these wealthy areas, the poor women who are not married have among them the highest proportion with local friends! If they have no husbands, they turn to the neighborhood for friends, even if it is a wealthy neighborhood. The solvent maintain friends beyond the neighborhood. (Similar results occur no matter what the wealth of the neighborhood.)

So far we have seen that the impact of neighborhood contextual dissonance is selective. It is a powerful factor in patterning the local friendships and the isolation from friends of working class men over sixty-five. But its influence on women of the same age is negligible. Therefore, we now examine separately the male and female members of the sample not yet sixty-five in order to ascertain whether the isolating effects of contextual dissonance are specific to one age category as well as to sex. For working class men under sixty-five, we find a somewhat muted set of variations in friendship patterns by neighborhood wealth. The effect of the local income context resembles what we found for older men. There are small proportional increases in isolation for the poor as neighborhood wealth increases and small decrements for the solvent. Likewise, proportionately more of the solvent and few of the poor have local friends in neighborhoods of increasing wealth. These differences are nowhere as pronounced as the ones we found for the aged males, but they go in the same direction, and the influence of dissonant and consonant contexts parallels what we found for the older men.

The younger working class women, however, are insensitive to neighborhood wealth if they are solvent themselves. Virtually identical proportions are isolated or have friends in the area at all levels of neighborhood wealth. Only poor females who live in the most dissonant economic contexts—in the most affluent neighborhoods—are relatively more isolated from friends and less integrated into a local friendship network than the rest. Incidentally, this high level of isolation of poor women in rich areas relative to poor women in poor neighborhoods does not depend upon marital status. In this sense, poor middle-aged women resemble middle-aged and old males: They are isolated by contextual dissonance.

The impact of neighborhood wealth, then, is felt mainly by the men and most strongly by the old men. Had we ventured a prediction before examining the data, doubtless we could have found a rationale for either this result or for its opposite—that the impact of neighborhood wealth would be strongest among the younger men. In the latter case, we might have argued from the premise that men under sixty-five are still engaged in work and are responsible for the support of their wives or other dependents or both. Therefore, they should be most subject to the assortative mechanisms through which social class position meshes with friendship patterns. It is apparent that reasoning from this or similar principles is unfounded. As far as patterns of friendship are concerned, the importance of personal income in ranking working class men relative to others is greater after the working years than before. Working class men once removed from their active roles in the economy interact with friends as if invidious economic criteria were the basis of friendship. Although this is clearly improbable on the level of individual motivation, it is quite plausible in another sense. The differential patterns which we observed in isolation and local friendship of the poor and of the solvent in dissonant and consonant economic contexts lead to the conclusion that structural contexts do combine powerfully with individual wealth to pattern friendships and the lack of them in old age according to inexorable economic criteria. Neighborhood economic consonance and dissonance stand for the ways in which the larger social class system impinges on this form of primary social participation for aged men and to a lesser degree for middle-aged men. The social class system in this sense can be viewed as one of the larger distributive systems of the society insofar as it plays a role in determining whether a social space, such as a neighborhood, will be class homogeneous or heterogeneous.

Thus, the friendship patterns imposed by the neighborhood context of wealth come about through the neighborhood balance of economic status-similars—the economic dissonance or consonance of the neighborhood. Additionally, if, on the one hand, the presence of economic status-similars by itself led to income status homophily, we would identify this fact as precisely the mechanism by which to elaborate the findings we have presented above. But if, on the other hand, economically heterophilous friendships were formed, they might present no theoretical difficulty in principle since heterophily may be interpreted as a form of pairing which can be "afforded" in a climate where the predominance of economic status-similars (contextual consonance) allows slippage—that is, allows cross-class, or cross-income level, affiliation to be maintained. Economic status heterophily may not be a threat to neighborhood norms in an area where there are few relatively wealthy people amid many poor or vice versa. The central point, however, is not the precise nature of the status match in friendship pairs. In fact, it is relatively unimportant for the purposes of this chapter that we be able to state whether the differential friendship patterns of poor and solvent working class people in similar neighborhoods are indeed of a particular assortative character—homophilous or heterophilous. That is a separate question with implications for role set theory and its filiation with a theory of social contexts. What is crucial here is that local assortative pairing, of whatever character, and isolation from friends as well are both functions of neighborhood economic consonance or dissonance in the working class—especially as applied to older men.

  Occupational Context. The preceding discussion, in its focus on income, singled out one among many class-related structural contexts which may influence friendship patterns. The potency of neighborhood contextual dissonance with respect to income may be unique. The close connection between income and style of life may create clearly visible similarities and differences among neighbors, facilitating the formation and maintenance of friendships according to income criteria. It is necessary, therefore, to examine other neighborhood contexts related to socioeconomic ranking, in particular, participation in the labor force and the occupational level at which that participation occurs, in order to ascertain the scope of the contextual effects deriving from the larger social class system. The underlying issue is the pervasiveness of class differences in their governance of friendship relations. If income level is the sole source of isolating contextual dissonance, then, in spite of the moderately strong correlation of income with other elements of socioeconomic rank, our judgment must be that class-linked contextual dissonance rests on a relatively superficial base. If, on the other hand, contextual dissonance which stems from differences in labor force participation and occupational level also isolates working class people, then there can be little doubt of the fundamentally divisive nature of social class differences in primary relations, especially in old age.

Confining our analysis to the friendship patterns of men, we examine two facets of the neighborhood occupational context: the extent to which the local area is supplied with people over forty-four who are in the labor force and the extent to which those over forty-four in the labor force hold blue-collar jobs.

Males under sixty-five live in a consonant context when their neighborhood is plentifully supplied with others of their approximate age level who work. If the effect of neighborhood labor force standing is similar to what we have just observed for neighborhood wealth, then isolation from friends should be least evident in the most consonant neighborhoods.[2] And solvent men, under sixty-five, are indeed isolated in smaller proportions in areas where working neighbors are in relatively plentiful supply. But poor men under sixty-five are not responsive to the labor force context. They are isolated from friends in exactly the same proportions no matter how many working neighbors they have. The nonresponsiveness of the middle-aged poor men to this class-linked neighborhood context is an extension of the incipient pattern noted above, where the poor men were simply less responsive than the solvent to neighborhood income level.

The lack of responsiveness to the labor force context holds also for poor men over sixty-five. The proportion of isolates among them remains constant at about a third no matter how many of their neighbors work. However, the solvent old men also resemble their younger counterparts in that the proportion of isolates among them decreases from over a half to slightly less than a third as the neighborhood becomes more heavily populated with working people. This finding runs counter to our expectation that consonant contexts have a minimizing effect on the level of isolation from friends. Although solvent old men in neighborhoods with larger numbers of workers live in dissonant labor force contexts, their rate of isolation is lower than in consonant ones, which, for them, would be neighborhoods with few workers. However, in dissonant neighbor-

---

[2] There are a small number of aged men in the labor force and a small number of retirees among those under sixty-five. However, controlling for labor force status does not alter the picture of the friendship patterns of those over and under sixty-five presented in this section.

hoods—those with larger numbers of workers—as large a proportion
of solvent old men maintain friendships beyond the neighborhood
(approximately 29 per cent) as are isolated (approximately 30
per cent). Possibly the solvent old men do not conceive of labor
force participation as the criterion for the kind of invidious comparison on which isolation may be based. And indeed, since their
rate of isolation is strongly responsive to income differences in the
neighborhood, as we have seen, and since their own solvency may
place them on a relatively equal footing with respect to income
with others who still earn wages, there may be little reason to
expect that contextual dissonance is promoted in neighborhoods
with large numbers of residents in the labor force.

When we turn to the neighborhood supply of workers who
are our respondents' occupational status-similars—that is, who hold
blue-collar jobs—the relationship between contextual consonance
and reduced isolation becomes fully reestablished. The more blue-
collar workers there are nearby, the smaller the proportion of
isolates there are among our male respondents and the larger the
proportion of them who have local friends. This is the case at all
age levels and also for the poor as well as for the solvent. But just
as we saw the solvent working class men to be more responsive
than the poor to the presence of working neighbors and more
responsive to neighborhood income differences, so now we also
observe a greater impact on the solvent than on the poor of the
presence of large numbers of workers with blue-collar jobs. Table 5
illustrates this finding for men sixty-five or more. Having larger
numbers of occupational peers reduces isolation and promotes local
friendship relations for poor and solvent alike. But solvent men are
generally more isolated and less integrated than the poor in identical
occupational contexts.

If men who are no longer employed are affected by the
neighborhood occupational context, we might expect younger men
who are still employed to be even more sensitive than those over
sixty-five to the lack of blue-collar peers in the neighborhood. On
these grounds, occupation ought to be most relevant to those still
working. But if there is reason to think that the occupational context of the neighborhood resembles in its effects the neighborhood

Table 5

Friendship Patterns of Poor and Solvent Males, Age Sixty-Five or More, by Number of Blue-Collar Workers Over Age Forty-Four in the Neighborhood

(in percentages)

Friendship Patterns	Number of Blue-Collar Workers Over Age 44 in the Neighborhood			
	0 to 15		16 or More	
	Poor (N = 73)	Solvent (N = 90)	Poor (N = 79)	Solvent (N = 83)
Isolates	41.1	52.2	27.8	26.5
Friends beyond the neighborhood	15.1	15.6	19.0	27.7
Friends within the neighborhood	43.8	32.2	53.2	45.8
Total	100.0	100.0	100.0	100.0

income structure, then we might assume that the occupational context wreaks similar but weaker effects on the middle-aged members of the sample than on the aged.

The data confirm that neighborhood occupational contexts resemble the contexts of neighborhood wealth in their effects. As with the old men, consonant occupational contexts reduce isolation and dissonant contexts increase it for these middle-aged males. Moreover, the impact of the local supply of blue-collar workers on isolation is not nearly as great for these younger men as it is for the older. For example, the difference in the proportions of the solvent young men who are isolated when they live in areas with high and with low concentrations of blue-collar neighbors is about 11 per cent. A glance at Table 5, however, reveals that the comparable spread between solvent old men living in areas with plentiful and in areas with scarce supplies of blue-collar neighbors is about 25 per cent. Likewise, the effect on isolation of having blue-collar neighbors is stronger among poor old men than among poor younger men. Furthermore, among these younger men, the poor remain less responsive to the occupational context than the solvent do. A slightly larger decline in the proportion who are isolated occurs among the solvent than among the poor when we compare those who live in neighborhoods containing small and large numbers of blue-collar workers. Again, this patterning of friendship relations parallels that which we found in the presence of income contexts.

The two general conclusions which emerge from these data on neighborhood occupational context are consistent with the findings on neighborhood wealth. First, the aged are affected more strongly than the middle aged and those out of the labor force more strongly than those remaining in it by aspects of the neighborhood context related to socioeconomic status. Second, the poor are less responsive than the solvent to the composition of the local social environment. But again, their lack of responsiveness works to their advantage. In dissonant contexts (few blue-collar neighbors), which promote isolation, smaller proportions of the poor than of the solvent are isolated. In consonant contexts (many blue-collar neighbors), which promote local friendships, larger proportions of the poor than of the solvent have friends within the neighborhood. The over-all similarity of the effects of income and of occupational con-

texts indicates that fundamental class differences rather than superficial style of life variations form the foundation of differential rates
of isolation from friends and of integration into local friendship
networks in the working class. The environment of local wealth
is only one among several factors tending to isolate working class
people. Equally as important is the lack of availability of class peers
in the occupational sense. The absence of manual workers from the
neighborhood places blue-collar and white-collar occupational differences into contrast.

When income is lessened and a job is relinquished, the
central roles of the retired revolve around family and neighborhood.
Is there reason then to expect that income level, blue-collar standing, and age/retirement become more rather than less powerfully
related to the wealth and occupational standing of neighbors and
to the maintenance of friendships among them? The meaning of
work, its income rewards, and the social class position of our
respondents are bound up in this question. They suggest some
admittedly speculative comments.

We must consider the simple notion of the activation of a
latent role. In old age, the companionship of fellow employees,
whether it was negligible or significant, is absent. A man's time is
spent at or near home, and he is exposed to neighbors more than
before. Thus, he becomes more vulnerable than before to the influence of neighborhood contexts; he is no longer a neighbor on weekends only. At this point social class factors become more rather
than less potent in governing friendship relations in the neighborhood—not that they were inoperative before, but rather that they
were not operative upon the man under sixty-five for so much of
his time or for so large a sector of his role set. That is, the transition to retirement is misconceived if it is thought of as a change to
a condition lacking a central role. The role of neighbor becomes
activated and replaces that of worker. It is not only a sequel to the
role of breadwinner but also has a set of role requirements (and
doubtless a process of socialization thereto—though we are not
prepared to investigate it in this study). The preceding analysis suggests that insofar as friendship is concerned, these role requirements
involve among other things governance of relations by such class-
related structures as the income and occupational contexts of the

neighborhood. Thus, economic influence on behavior does not cease in old age and retirement. Of course, the socioeconomic context is not the only crucial factor involved in friendship relations. But the analysis so far indicates that it is certainly one important factor in patterning the friendships of male working class people in old age. We may well divest ourselves, then, of the idea of old age in the working class as a social limbo, of retirement as a beginning of an ineluctable separation or disengagement of the aging man from society and correlatively of the relaxation of the influence of his socioeconomic environment upon him.

Also we may discard the notion that the social costs or social deprivations associated with poverty (especially in old age) deny the poor, as compared with those not poor, companionship because they are poor and because they are surrounded by affluence. As far as friendship relations are concerned, these are unprofitable concepts. Nothing in our data so far supports such a notion. Rather, the contrary seems to be true. These findings suggest that poor people who have held blue-collar jobs for most of their lives cope more successfully with the absence of their occupational peers and integrate themselves more thoroughly into informal social networks in the presence of their occupational peers than do solvent blue-collar men. And where their neighbors differ in income standing, fewer of them suffer from isolation, and more of them than of their solvent counterparts manage to find friends. Proportionately more of the poor than of the solvent have the ability, apparently, to integrate themselves into socioeconomically dissonant neighborhood contexts. A low level of income reward from a lifetime of work may facilitate rather than hinder the development of an orientation enabling the poor to cope effectively with neighbors (rather than to withdraw or to maintain friendships outside the neighborhood) in spite of class pressures which affect their solvent age peers more strongly.

We can now see more clearly the meaning of the small difference in isolation reported earlier in this chapter between the poor and the solvent themselves. Our results so far clearly indicate that if the poor and the solvent were both living in socioeconomically identical neighborhood contexts in equal proportions, more of the solvent than of the poor would be isolated. And since we have found that dissonance produces isolation, the true size of the relationship between poverty and isolation must be concealed by the skewed residential distribution of the poor toward dissonant neighborhoods. This distribution inflates, somewhat, the crude rate of isolation of the poor for the entire sample and suppresses somewhat the differences which would exist were the poor distributed more evenly over the range of neighborhoods sampled.

RACIAL CONTEXT

To complete this examination of class-linked structural contexts and their effects on friendship patterns, we turn now to an analysis of the impact of race on isolation from friends and integration into local friendship networks. The racial composition of the neighborhood and the race of our respondents are ascriptive factors which do not directly reflect the achieved class position of the members of the sample or their neighbors in quite the same sense as do income and occupation. But nevertheless the racial context is by extension one aspect of the socioeconomic character of the local environment which has implications for the economic standing of a neighborhood and for the status honor evaluations of its residents. As such, it presents the population of the local area with a basis for invidious comparison which should resemble, in its impact on friendship patterns, the effects of income and occupational contexts. We expect, then, that racial contexual dissonance will isolate the members of our white working class sample. And as we found in our examination of income and occupational contexts, we expect the solvent to be more responsive than the poor to this dissonance.

We measure the racial composition of the neighborhood by the proportion of Negro households it contains. Whether this measure or the number of Negro households is employed, the configuration of friendship patterns remains the same. That is, the racial balance of the neighborhood is neither more nor less consequential for isolation and friendship than is the absolute number of Negroes in it.

The patterning of friendship in racially segregated and integrated neighborhoods is shown in Table 6 for old working class people. Men and women are combined in Table 6 since their friendship patterns are similarly influenced by the neighborhood racial context. The presence of Negro households in a neighborhood is associated with increased isolation and reduced local friendships for both poor and solvent. However, the magnitude of these differences is considerably greater for the solvent than for the poor. Whether their friends are Negroes or whether the aged poor are to be viewed as an embattled group which maintains a high level of local friendships with whites in the face of (or perhaps because of)' the invasion of their area by Negroes is quite beside the point. Whatever the mechanism, the white aged poor do not abandon the neighborhood as a source of friends nearly to the extent that their solvent age peers do when the racial balance becomes increasingly weighted toward the Negro side.

For working class people under sixty-five we observe again a differential impact of racially dissonant contexts. The younger poor and solvent alike, in neighborhoods with up to 50 per cent of the households containing Negroes, are isolated in greater proportions than they are in all-white neighborhoods, but the isolation of the poor increases only slightly, while that of the solvent increases appreciably. But in the areas with the largest proportions of Negro households, the level of isolation for both the poor and the solvent younger working class people drops down to slightly below what it was in the all-white neighborhoods! And when the local friendships of younger people in all-white and integrated neighborhoods are considered we find a parallel difference between the poor and the solvent.

Part of the explanation for this pattern of isolation is the greater opportunity for contact with Negro neighbors on the part of those who do not work. Among the younger people, the wives are the one segment of the population most closely bound to the neighborhood since the men and many of the unmarried women work. And integrated neighborhoods do increase the isolation and reduce the rate of local friendships of the younger wives, both poor and solvent, to about the same degree. The racially dissonant context is not so salient for the younger men and hence has no appreciable influence on their friendship patterns. But among those over sixty-five, neither the men nor the women work. The isolation of males and females, both poor and solvent, is greater in inte-

Table 6

Friendship Patterns of the Poor and Solvent, Age Sixty-Five or More, by Proportion of Negro Households in the Neighborhood
(in percentages)[a]

Friendship Patterns	Poor			Solvent		
	Proportion Negro Households in Neighborhood					
	0 (N = 249)	0.01 to 0.50 (N = 76)	0.51 to 0.99 (N = 44)	0 (N = 234)	0.01 to 0.50 (N = 42)	0.51 to 0.99 (N = 23)
Isolates	28.5	46.0	47.7	33.8	64.3	56.5
Friends beyond the neighborhood	17.3	7.9	6.8	20.9	9.5	26.1
Friends within the neighborhood	54.2	46.0	45.5	45.3	26.2	17.4
Total	100.0	100.0	100.0	100.0	100.0	100.0

[a] Percentages may not add to 100 because of rounding.

grated than in all-white neighborhoods and greater in neighborhoods with high than in those with low proportions of Negro households. Thus, the effects of the neighborhood racial context parallel in broad outline those of the income and occupational contexts.

CONCLUSION

This chapter began with a general inquiry about the relation of poverty and old age to isolation from friends in the urban white working class. It soon became apparent that poverty and age in themselves are unrelated to isolation from friends. Placing other research on the working class in juxtaposition to the finding that most of our respondents have friends living on their own block suggested that the social composition of the neighborhood is central to interaction among friends and to the lack of it. In this light, we examined in detail the neighborhood context—the social composition of the blocks on which the subjects of this study reside.

Though it was not reported earlier, an analysis was attempted of the effect on friendship patterns of neighborhood contexts for three age groupings (sixty-five or more, fifty-five to sixty-four, fifty-four or less) without regard to poverty or solvency, and this effect was found to be negligible. The reason becomes apparent when we consider the influence of neighborhood contexts on the poor and the solvent separately within each age grouping. The same context often affects the friendship patterns of the poor and of the solvent in opposite ways, so that for any given age level, the differences in friendship patterns of the poor and solvent tend to cancel each other when the two income groups were combined.

The distinguishing feature of the neighborhood contexts is their connection with the socioeconomic standing of the people who live in the neighborhood. The solvent working class people of our study are more responsive than the poor to neighborhood contexts related to socioeconomic rank. Moreover, when the friendship patterns of working class people, whether poor or solvent, are affected by the neighborhood context, these effects are of an orderly nature: Neighborhood contextual dissonance increases the possibility that an individual will be isolated from friends, and neighborhood contextual consonance increases the probability that an individual will be integrated into a neighborhood friendship network. Not surprisingly, then, those class-linked neighborhood contextual factors which increase the proportion of the isolated poor tend to have the opposite effect on the solvent, at a given age level.

When the poor and the solvent are both living in dissonant neighborhood contexts, if those contexts happen to be related to socioeconomic standing, proportionately fewer of the poor than of the solvent are isolated. Yet the residential distribution of the poor, as compared with that of the solvent people in our sample, is sharply skewed toward the contextually dissonant neighborhood socioeconomic contexts. Hence the lack of difference in the proportion of isolates among all the poor and the solvent, which we remarked upon at the outset of our investigation, is in a sense a spurious nonassociation. Were the poor and the solvent distributed over the residential areas of the city so that equal proportions of them lived in contextually dissonant neighborhoods, then the solvent doubtless would be significantly more isolated than the poor at a given age level. However, in Philadelphia the poor are not so distributed.

Additionally, the effects of neighborhood social contexts are most strongly manifest among old people (over sixty-five), and among old men at that. In other words, age in itself is relevant to patterns of friendship and isolation from friends only insofar as it signifies a transformation from the role of breadwinner to that of neighbor. And this change typically takes place for men upon reaching sixty-five. When this role transformation occurs, neighborhood contextual dissonance and consonance come into play more fully than before in determining the patterns of friendship and isolation from friends of poor and solvent working class people.

Family-Cycle
Context of Friendship

A quintessence even from
nothingnesse,
From dull privations, and
leane emptinesse

JOHN DONNE
*A nocturnall upon S. Lucies day,
Being the shortest day*

55

n this chapter we analyze selected dimensions of neighborhood social structure which do not pertain to socioeconomic hierarchy. We turn here from the class context of social affiliations to view the members of our sample in the perspective of their age and of the relationship of age-connected dimensions of neighborhood social structure to friendship and isolation from friends. Of course, we do not ignore the distinction between poor and solvent working class people which played such a large role in the analysis of the preceding chapter and upon which hinged the strength and direction of the effects of neighborhood consonance and dissonance. But we continue our investigation of the structural grounds of social isolation from friends from different initial premises. We conceive of the members of our sample primarily as old people now, and from the numerous dimensions of neighborhood social structure which can be analyzed, we select those which seem to have an especially close bearing on age itself—the age structure of the neighborhoods, the marital contexts, the size of families, and the size of individual households. As we proceed we at appropriate points assess whether these aspects of neighborhood social structure are independent of the class-linked dimensions of the local context of friendship investigated in the preceding chapter. And finally, we bring together the analysis of this chapter and that of Chapter Two by considering the relationship of class and family life-cycle social contexts to determine their combined effect on friendship and isolation from friends and whether they work at cross-purposes in this regard.

By proceeding in this manner we retain the main features of the analytic perspective employed in our examination of class-linked structural contexts. That is, we expect that contextual dissonance will isolate our respondents from local friendships and that contextual consonance will result in the maintenance of friendships with neighbors. However, in transferring the contextual dissonance rule from class to family-cycle contexts we make a heuristic assumption. In advance of the evidence, we are in principle invoking the parity of structural contexts with respect to patterns of affiliation. When, in the case of class-linked contexts, the dis-

sonance consisted in the invidious contrast between the individual
and an enveloping grouping of neighbors, the isolating effects seemed
understandable at an almost intuitive level. Decades of research
have accustomed us to accept as virtually inevitable the tendency
of class-dissimilars not to congregate. But in contexts which refer
to family cycle, where the relationship of dissonance may consist
in a difference of age or marital status, the lack of an inherently
invidious basis of contrast stands in the way of understanding how
dissonance in this sense may result in isolation. For the conception
of dissonance linked to the family cycle refers directly neither to the
competitive, achievement-oriented criteria assumed by the notion
of class-linked contextual dissonance nor, to take another kind of
example entirely, to the incipiently conflictual criteria of religious
contextual dissonance. But competitive or conflictual social relationships are not the only ones which should be conceived of as
isolating. As Weber (1968, p. 361) insightfully realized, whatever
form neighborly proximity may take, "not only the fleeting 'to-
getherness' in streetcar, railroad or hotel, but also the enduring
one in an apartment house is by and large oriented toward maintaining the greatest possible *distance* in spite of (or because)' of
the physical proximity. . . ." The neighborhood context as a social
entity may be conducive to social isolation among its residents on
the basis of any number of criteria of dissonance.

What may be at issue is not the isolating effect of family-
cycle neighborhood contextual dissonance but rather whether all
subpopulations within a neighborhood are equally affected by
family-cycle contexts. In the preceding chapter, we saw that two
such subpopulations, the poor and the solvent, were not equally
affected. To be sure, class-linked contextual dissonance isolated all
males within a given age range, but it isolated the solvent more
than the poor. This finding signifies the variation from grouping
to grouping in the class system concerning the operation of invidious
norms in patterns of primary social participation. Of this variation
there was never any doubt, but it was the task of that chapter to
demonstrate that the variations operate through structural contexts,
to establish the kinds of variation which do occur, and to locate
precisely at what points they occur. Likewise, the task of this chapter
is to specify the variation which occurs in patterns of friendship

behavior because of the operation of noninvidious norms concerning the family and the family cycle.

In specifying this variation, we ask if the poor are more or less responsive than the solvent to structural contexts which have little connection with socioeconomic hierarchy. At issue here is the fundamental nature of at least one aspect of poverty in the segment of our society sampled in this study. Are the social relations of the poor or at least that aspect which pertains to friendship a variant of or an alternative to the larger working class pattern of affiliation? This is not a question of the existence of a "culture of poverty." That issue rests on kinds of evidence other than the interaction patterns of the poor and those not poor and is not under study here. Rather, we are concerned with the flexibility of the class system and the articulation of its parts in a structural sense. The variance in rates of isolation and integration within class contexts, which we have already seen, indicates the pervasiveness of social class as the structural context of friendship. But until we have examined directly the influence on friendship patterns of structural contexts unrelated to social class, we cannot judge whether there is an alternative pattern of primary participation in the poverty-stricken segment of the working class.

Should the evidence of the following pages indicate that the poor continue to be less responsive than the solvent to the isolating effects of dissonant structural contexts, this time contexts based on family-cycle criteria, then we may suppose that the social system of the poor is a structural variant of the main working class type insofar as primary participation is concerned. The poor will have been shown to be isolated by this form of structural dissonance too, but simply to a lesser degree than others. However, if the poor are more responsive than the solvent to the isolating effects of family-cycle contextual dissonance and to the integrating effects of family-cycle contextual consonance, then we must seriously consider the existence of an alternative system of primary social participation for poor as over and against other working class people. This would be evidence of a rather compelling order that working class systems of social affiliation are not only flexible (in that they admit of considerable variation along socioeconomically hierarchical dimensions) but also complex, that is, they permit some degree of articulation among the different structural contexts of friendship patterns. Stated more generally, this response pattern would be presumptive evidence of the selectivity of contextual effects on primary participation. As such, it would illustrate one way in which the integration of disparate subgroupings into larger social systems occur and at the same time would show what conditions lead to the failure of such integration.

FAMILY-CYCLE CONTEXTS

We turn to a consideration of some aspects of the neighborhood as a social context which are on the face of it unrelated to the socioeconomic character of the neighborhood population. In one way or another, these contextual aspects of the local area seem to be connected with the stage in the family cycle at which the residents of the neighborhood have arrived. In examining the effects of these contexts on patterns of friendship, we are looking for parallels and disparities in our findings here as compared with those of the preceding chapter. That is, we pay particular attention to whether, at a given age level, the poor are more responsive than the solvent to the effects of neighborhood contextual dissonance and consonance. And also, we note whether family-cycle contexts, like class-linked contexts, are mainly confined to the aged in their effects.

Two aspects of neighborhood age structure concern us here: the average age of the neighbors as a whole, indicated by a measure of the central tendency of the age distribution of its residents; and the concentration in the neighborhood of residents of specific ages, particularly those who correspond in years to our respondents, indicated by the proportion of all residents who are at a particular age level.

Looking at the friendship patterns of those respondents less than sixty-five, we find, as we did for most of the class-linked contexts in the preceding chapter, that for these middle-aged working class people, both the poor and the solvent, there are no contextual effects due to the mean age of the neighbors. The friendships of those under sixty-five are similarly patterned whether the mean age of the neighborhood is high or low.

But working class men sixty-five or older are affected by the over-all age level of their neighborhoods. Moreover, for these old

working class people, the effect of the neighborhood age context
in terms of strength and direction depends on whether they are
poor or solvent. In glancing at the proportion of isolates among
poor old men in Table 7, we see that it is progressively lower the
higher the mean age of their neighborhood. Thus, the contextual
dissonance principle holds in their case when the criterion is age.
But Table 7 tells quite a different story about the solvent old
men. They have a larger proportion of isolates among them in
consonant than in dissonant contexts. But in the oldest neighborhoods of all, their level of isolation drops somewhat—yet not quite
back to where it was in the youngest, the most dissonant, neighborhoods. The percentages seem to go in the wrong direction. Although
this essentially ambiguous finding may appear to be an exception
to the general rule, the differences in the proportions of solvent
old isolates in neighborhoods of varying age are not statistically
significant. Moreover, the curvilinearity of the relationship prevents
us from making an argument based on unidirectionality.

Table 7 also illustrates that the contextual dissonance principle holds in a parallel manner for local friendships. For the poor,
age dissonance results in smaller proportions of friendships in the
local area than does age consonance. For the solvent old men
the age of the neighborhood has the opposite effect on local friendship. But note that although in the oldest neighborhoods few solvent
old men find local friends, a large proportion of them have friends
who live elsewhere, whereas almost none of the poor old men have
friends beyond the neighborhood in these areas.

The apparent failure of the contextual dissonance and
consonance rule to hold for solvent old men is repeated in the case
of some of the women. The aged poor wives are less isolated in old
than in young neighborhoods, and more of them have neighborhood
friends in old than in young neighborhoods. But the proportion of
isolated solvent old wives remains the same no matter what the age
level of the neighborhood.

Another concern with the neighborhood structural context
of age is also illuminated by Table 7. Do the poor experience the
similarities and differences in age between themselves and their
neighbors in the same way that they experience economic similarities
and differences? The preceding chapter demonstrated that the

Table 7

FRIENDSHIP PATTERNS OF POOR AND SOLVENT MALES, AGE SIXTY-FIVE OR MORE, BY MEAN AGE OF NEIGHBORHOOD
(in percentages)[a]

Friendship Patterns	Poor			Solvent		
	Mean Age of Neighborhood					
	0 to 34 Years (N = 61)	35 to 44 Years (N = 58)	45 or More Years (N = 33)	0 to 34 Years (N = 73)	35 to 44 Years (N = 69)	45 or More Years (N = 31)
Isolates	41.0	31.0	27.3	31.5	49.3	38.7
Friends beyond the neighborhood	24.6	15.5	6.1	19.2	20.3	29.0
Friends within the neighborhood	34.4	53.4	66.7	49.3	30.4	32.3
Total	100.0	100.0	100.0	100.0	100.0	100.0

[a] Percentages may not add to 100 because of rounding.

solvent are more responsive than the poor to contexts related to socioeconomic status. We find a reversal of this situation when we deal with neighborhood contexts which are prima facie unrelated to socioeconomic standing. In Table 7, the proportional difference in isolation from friends and integration into local friendship networks which is revealed by contrasting the neighborhoods with oldest and those with the youngest people is greater for the poor than for the solvent. The poor are thus more responsive than the solvent to contextual factors not linked to social class. And the lack of contextual effect of neighborhood age on the solvent old wives, accompanied by the usual isolating effect of (age) dissonance on the poor old wives, seems to lend additional strength to the view that the patterning of friendship relations by non-economic contexts is part of an alternate system of local social participation in the working class.

The mean age of the neighborhood is only one possible measure of neighborhood age context. It can be supplemented by indicators which focus more directly upon the presence of age peers. The friendship relations of working class people who live in areas with higher than usual concentrations of the aged may cast further light on the contrasting patterns of isolation of the poor and of the solvent old men and wives. In neighborhoods with a high probability for contact with age peers, old people may exhibit higher local friendship rates by virtue of the increased availability of age status-similars. The proportion of persons in the respondent's block who are sixty-five or more indicates age concentration. However, very few neighborhoods have as much as 40 per cent of their residents sixty-five or over. Hence, few aged members of our working class sample dwell in such areas (eighteen poor old men and ten solvent old men). But we will discuss the data in spite of the exceedingly small numbers because of the theoretical importance of the issue.

Does age contextual dissonance, measured now by the concentration of the elderly in the neighborhood, continue to isolate the poor but not the solvent when we focus directly on the local supply of age peers of our respondents? The answer, as revealed in Table 8, is both yes and no. Neighborhoods which are dissonant in this respect tend to isolate the poor old men but not the solvent. But for the very small number of people in our sample who live in neighborhoods with the highest concentration of older persons, the reversal of this pattern is suggestive. Contrary to what we would expect, these areas do not necessarily result in either lower proportions of isolates or higher proportions of local friends for the older working class people who live in them than do the neighborhoods sparsely supplied. Table 8 shows that up to a point the isolation of the poor declines with increasing proportions of their age peers in the neighborhood. This finding conforms to what we observed above (in Table 7) when we employed mean age as the indicator of neighborhood age structure. But when the concentration of the aged in the neighborhood reaches 40 per cent, isolation of the poor old men rises to its highest level! For solvent old men, we saw that when the mean age of the neighborhood was the indicator of age structure (Table 7), the proportion of isolates among them rose in neighborhoods of increasing age, but in neighborhoods with the oldest people it fell back to a somewhat lower level. Now we see that when the concentration of people sixty-five and over in the neighborhood increases, the level of isolation of solvent old men also rises. But in the neighborhoods with the highest concentration of all, the isolation of the solvent old men falls to about as low a level as in the neighborhoods with the smallest concentration of aged residents.

In addition, the poor are more responsive than the solvent to fluctuations in the neighborhood concentration of age peers. Whether the comparison between the poor and the solvent is based on the difference in proportion of isolates in neighborhoods of low versus intermediate concentrations of age peers or in neighborhoods of low versus high concentrations of age peers, a greater proportional change from one neighborhood to another characterizes the poor. Again, this change conforms to the one we found when the age structure of the neighborhood was measured by mean age.

Let us turn from isolation to local friendships. In Table 7 as the age of the neighbors increased, so did the proportion of the poor with local friends. But when we employ a more specific measure of age concentration we see, in Table 8, that old poor men do not have the highest proportions of local friends in areas where the concentration of their age peers is highest. But for the

Table 8

FRIENDSHIP PATTERNS OF POOR AND SOLVENT MALES, AGE SIXTY-FIVE OR MORE, BY PROPORTION OF PERSONS IN THE NEIGHBORHOOD WHO ARE SIXTY-FIVE YEARS OR MORE

(in percentages)

Friendship Patterns	Poor			Solvent		
	Proportion of Neighborhood 65 or More					
	0 to 0.19 (N = 105)	0.20 to 0.39 (N = 29)	0.40 or More (N = 18)	0 to 0.19 (N = 117)	0.20 to 0.39 (N = 46)	0.40 or More (N = 10)
Isolates	37.1	17.2	44.4	37.6	45.7	40.0
Friends beyond the neighborhood	20.0	13.8	5.6	19.7	23.9	30.0
Friends within the neighborhood	42.9	69.0	50.0	42.7	30.4	30.0
Total	100.00	100.0	100.0	100.0	100.0	100.0

solvent old men we find much the same pattern of local friendships no matter which indicator we use. The greatest proportion of these relatively well-to-do old men have local friendships when they live in neighborhoods with the lowest concentration of their age peers or in neighborhoods with lowest mean age.

And again, the aged poor are more responsive to the concentration of older people in their neighborhood with respect to local friendships. The difference in the proportion of old people with local friends as between areas with low and intermediate concentration of age peers is greater for the poor than for the solvent old people—in part because of the willingness or ability of the solvent old people to participate in friendly relations with people beyond the neighborhood—a factor observable in Table 7 also.

Focusing on old working class wives, we find no startling differences in friendship patterns from what has been noted above. The isolation of solvent old wives remains at the same level in all neighborhoods, while that of the poor old wives falls in areas of higher concentration of the aged. The proportion of poor old wives with local friends rises with increasing neighborhood concentration of the aged, and the proportion of solvent old wives with local friends falls under the same circumstances. But many of these solvent old married women have friends elsewhere.

To this point we have found, first, that the friendship patterns of large elements of the working class population being studied are simply unaffected by certain aspects of neighborhood age structure. Those unaffected are mainly the young working class respondents. Their lack of responsiveness to the age context of the neighborhood perhaps is an artifact of the measures of neighborhood age structure. So far, these measures concentrate on the oldest residents of the neighborhood (proportion sixty-five or more) or else are particularly sensitive to the extremes of the local age distribution (mean age of the neighborhood inhabitants). This notion is plausible only on the assumption that the friends of the young are themselves chosen from among the young, and hence the presence of the aged would be unlikely to make much difference. We discuss the effects of the presence of younger neighbors shortly.

Second, however, the presence of old people in their neighborhoods is expected to and does influence the friendship patterns

of the aged. But clear divergences have emerged between the poor
and the solvent old people who live in areas of similar age structure.
The poor are more responsive than the solvent to the age context.
Also, the aged poor have larger proportions of friends and smaller
proportions of isolates among themselves in neighborhoods with old
people. But the friendship patterns of the solvent old people run
counter to those of their poor peers and to our expectation that
contextual dissonance and isolation are positively associated. In
general, and with the proviso that these differences are small, the
solvent have smaller proportions of friends and larger proportions
of isolated people among themselves when they live in areas with
old neighbors.

Is it, however, the age composition of the neighborhood or
the income level of neighbors which accounts for the contrasting
patterns of friendship of the poor and the solvent? The correlation
between mean age of neighbors and mean family income in the
neighborhood is negative, −0.68. In consequence, the aged poor in
neighborhoods heavily populated by old people are in doubly consonant neighborhood contexts—they live among income- as well
as among age status-similars. Thus, the findings above are plausible:
The higher the mean age of the neighborhood, the more the aged
poor resemble its residents in income as well as age and the more
likely is the occurrence of friendly interaction in the neighborhood.
But although solvent old people in neighborhoods with relatively
older inhabitants by definition live among age peers, they also live
among neighbors who are likely to be poor and hence dissimilar
with respect to income level. In one respect they live in a consonant and in another in a dissonant neighborhood context. From
what, then, are the solvent isolated in such neighborhoods: their
neighbors' ages or their neighbors' poverty?

If the poverty of neighbors most affects the solvent people's
friendships even though the neighborhood is populated by relatively
many others who are old like themselves, then we should observe
that in neighborhoods which are both old and relatively wealthy, a
larger proportion of our solvent aged respondents should have local
friends than in neighborhoods which are old but relatively poor.
However, we can find little support for the idea that age is
spuriously related to friendships. The difference in local friendship

among solvent old people (men and women) in old-poor and in old-wealthy neighborhoods is slight. The age level of the neighborhood has, then, an independent relationship to friendship patterns for both the poor and the solvent and also as far as both local friendships and isolation are concerned. And the direction of this relationship indicates that old people who are solvent are integrated into a local social system of informal affiliations mainly in a neighborhood setting characteristic of a younger, more economically involved stage of life. Their social distance from the young is probably less and their integration into a normative order characteristic of younger age cohorts is probably greater than would be the case among the aged working class poor.

Third, and perhaps most provocative of all, our examination of those admittedly few cases in which old people live in areas with unusually high concentrations of the aged reveals an unexpected reversal of the pattern observed before in this analysis of neighborhood age context. Instead of smaller proportions of the aged poor becoming isolated and larger proportions of them maintaining local friendships as the proportion of their age peers in the neighborhood reaches its highest point, just the opposite occurs. Under these seemingly most favorable circumstances for friendship, the highest proportion of aged poor men are isolated, and the proportion with local friends drops almost to the level at which it is found in neighborhoods with the lowest concentration of old people, and similarly for those old solvent people living in neighborhoods plentiful in age peers. The trend of increasing proportions of isolates in areas progressively better supplied with age peers is reversed; and the drop in the proportions of solvent old people with local friends comes to a halt.

The number of cases involved is too small for further analysis. But their implications, tentative though they may be, deserve heeding. These data suggest that the efficacy for friendship relations of very high age-peer concentration should not be presumed in all cases and under all conditions. Rosow's (1967) evidence that such concentration promotes age status homophily (see Chapter Two) was derived from as specialized a population as ours, but a different one sociologically. And his age and class distinctions do not correspond to our age and income distinctions. Further, his "neighborhood" consisted of an apartment house, ours mainly of a city block of row houses. Thus, although we have two basically noncomparable findings (and hence they are not worthy of the claim that they are contradictory), nevertheless we would hazard a guess about age concentration which is at least partially at odds with previous research, in order to keep future options open for more comprehensive and definitive work. That is, the concentration of age peers which is optimal for local friendship depends on the economic standing of the persons whose affiliations are in question. By and large, for the aged poor, the concentration of age peers optimal for maintaining local friendships and correlatively for lack of isolation from friends is not the highest possible concentration, and for the aged solvent it even may be a relatively lower concentration than that. And although there is scant evidence for it here, age-homophilous friendships may be as much, if not more, a function of income level as of the opportunity presented by concentrations of age-similars in the local environment.

If, to continue in this speculative vein for the moment, these suppositions concerning age concentration and friendship turn out to be true, it may be because age homophily is not completely characteristic of the local affiliations of old people, perhaps because some of the aged place a low value on being old. For some of the aged, then, neighborhoods which supply a heavy concentration of age peers at the same time supply a basis for the devaluation of a presently held status. In such a situation, old people who place a low value on being thought old, by themselves or others, can either isolate themselves from all friendship relations or seek more compatible affiliations beyond the neighborhood or ignore age as a criterion of friendship and maintain their social relationships with neighbors on the basis of different criteria. In Table 8 some one or more of these options appear to have been exercised by the solvent old people faced with increasingly higher concentrations of the aged in their neighborhoods. The proportion of them who have friends beyond the neighborhood rises steadily with the increase in concentration of old people in the local area. Accompanying this flight from the neighborhood as a source of friends is a steady decline in the proportion with friends in the neighborhood. Further, the variation in proportion of isolates in neighborhoods with different concentrations of the aged is not particularly large and in fact is almost irrelevant. Moreover, we may maintain that the pattern of friendship relations displayed by the solvent old men in Table 8 or elements of this pattern represent a working class norm. That is, age (and perhaps also other factors related to family cycle)' typically is not the basis of assortative pairing among older, retired working class people, and its chief effects, where there is high age contextual consonance, may not become manifest in isolation rates but rather in lowered rates of local friendship as a result of their having gone outside the neighborhood for friendly social intercourse, for to associate with the very old is demeaning. The American culture does not direct that old age be looked upon with reverence and esteem.

But the poor old men exhibit an alternate form of primary participation insofar as friendship is concerned. It may be based on a higher valuation of old age per se than can be found among the solvent or than is typical of the working class in general. The data on poor old men, in Table 8, suggest that for some of them affiliation with old people may not be demeaning. The poor do not maintain friendships beyond the neighborhood when concentrations of the aged reach very high levels. Fully 50 per cent of them have local friends under these conditions, which is considerably larger than the proportion of solvent old men who have local friends under the identical neighborhood concentration of elderly. Yet at the same time, a substantial proportion of the aged poor in these neighborhoods remain isolated. Perhaps counternormative patterns of affiliation are not easily maintained by all, and we have here a residual proportion of the poor old men who conform in behavior to the modal cultural orientation.

But let us turn from what are at this stage admittedly speculative comments about age concentration and friendship relations to additional data which may clarify our remarks. When we look at the local concentration of people in the middle years, between the ages of forty-five and sixty-four, a parallel patterning of friendship relations emerges. Moreover, the friendship patterns of poor and solvent working class men and women are similar at all age levels. At this point, then, we are discussing the entire sample. The solvent working class people are virtually unresponsive to the neighborhood concentration of middle-aged people. One-third of the solvent are isolated from friends no matter what concentration of neighbors age forty-five to sixty-four exists in their local area. And slightly more than 40 per cent of the solvent have local friends no matter what the neighborhood age concentration of people in their middle years. The responsiveness of the poor to the concentration of middle-aged neighbors is revealed by the declining proportion of isolates among them and the increasing proportion of those with local friends in neighborhoods with progressively greater concentrations of people aged forty-five to sixty-four. Where the concentration of neighbors in the middle years is 19 per cent or less, about 42 per cent of the poor are isolated; the proportion of isolates declines to 29 per cent where the concentration of middle-aged neighbors is 40 per cent or more. And the proportion of poor people integrated into the neighborhood through friendship rises from 45 to about 59 per cent with increasing concentration of middle-aged neighbors. These relationships run in the expected direction. And this pattern of differential impact of neighborhood concentration of people age forty-five to sixty-four on the friendship patterns of the poor and the solvent is universal among our respondents. It holds, as we have said, without exception for all ages, for married and unmarried respondents, for males and females, and for the poor and the solvent when age is held constant. It signifies that solvent people's patterns of friendship are immune to the concentration of middle-aged neighbors in their locality. This immunity is of a piece with our finding, above, in Table 8, that the integration of old solvent people into local friendship networks decreases when they live in areas where other old people are highly concentrated. In both that and the present instance, friendship relations of the solvent either are divorced from or are irrelevant to age grading at the local level.

But all poor people, the middle aged and the elderly, are somewhat affected by the concentration of the middle aged in the neighborhood. This is a further indication that an alternate system of friendship relations prevails for poor working class people. For the poor, the presence in high concentrations of people of their own or adjacent age is not only a criterion of local affiliation but also a condition which reduces isolation and increases the rate of local friendships. In general, the direction of these relationships conforms to what we found when the mean age of the neighborhood was the measure of age context and when we observed the local concentration of the very old in the neighborhood. Thus evidence begins to accumulate that while class-linked contexts pattern friendships for the poor to a lesser extent than they do for solvent working class people, those contexts related to family cycle do influence poor people's friendship patterns but do not affect those of solvent working class people.

Marriage. We consider now the presence of nuclear families in the neighborhood and its relation to patterns of friendship. Neighborhoods are characterized here by the proportion of their residents who are married. People below fifty-five are unaffected by the marital composition of the neighborhood. They have the same proportion of isolates and the same proportion integrated into local friendship networks regardless of the neighborhood marital composition. And the poor do not differ from the solvent in this respect. However, the effects of the marital composition of the neighborhood are seen in the friendship patterns of older working class people. Among men and women over sixty-five there is a clear differential between the friendship patterns of the poor and those of the solvent in neighborhoods of varying marital composition. The effect of increasing proportions of married neighbors is to increase the proportion of isolates among the poor old people—from 31 per cent in areas where 67 per cent or less of the population is married to 49 per cent in areas where 82 per cent or more of the neighbors are married—and to decrease the proportion among them with friends in the neighborhood—from about 59 to 35 per cent. But solvent old people are isolated to about the same degree and have neighborhood friends in approximately equal proportions in neighborhoods of all kinds. The marital context of the neighborhood, then, affects the poor, but the solvent old people are unresponsive to it.

These findings are not a function of the marital status of the respondents themselves. At each age and income level, both the married and those who are not presently married, the men as well as the women, display the same patterns of local friendship and isolation. Therefore, it is not the companionship of a spouse which insulates people from loneliness and leads them to ignore the neighborhood as a source of friendships. If aged poor people are not married they are as isolated as their married peers, and their isolation is positively associated with the presence of married couples in the neighborhood. These findings are also not a function of the retirement of husbands, which tends to occur at or near sixty-five. Precisely the pattern of isolation and affiliation described above occurs among working class people between fifty-five and sixty-four, among whom the overwhelming majority of males are still in the labor force.

There are strong similarities between the patterning of friendships by the marital context observed here and by the age context discussed above. The marital structure of the neighborhood and the age structure are not contexts to which solvent old working class people respond. The poor are isolated in greatest proportion in neighborhoods with low mean age and in neighborhoods where the proportion of married people is high. (As we would suspect, there is a negative correlation, −0.46, between age and proportion of people in the neighborhood who are married.) And the largest proportions of the poor have friends in neighborhoods where the mean age is high and the proportion of married people is low. The nature of these neighborhood parameters which thus affect the poor indicates that the contextual dissonance or consonance which constitutes an alternate system of primary social participation is not made up of relationships defined by particular marital statuses, such as widowhood, which provide a direct, clearly circumscribed status similarity among neighbors. But the alternate structural context of friendship for the poor must be thought of as an environment in which many others have reached a certain stage of the life cycle and of the family cycle broadly defined. The match between these poor men and women past fifty-five and their neighbors doubtless rests on a broad similarity of experience and common norms, such as launching of children into the occupational world, retirement or impending retirement, and problems of dependency which may accompany old age. Whatever their manifest content, these family-cycle and life-cycle similarities engage the poor and fail to engage their economically more successful age peers as criteria of neighborhood interaction. The fact that there is no con-

venient and clear label for the status defined by these family- and
life-cycle attributes—as there is, by contrast, for income, occupational, and racial status—reflects the inadequacy of our conceptual-
ization of the stages of aging. The demonstrable reality of these
stages of later life in defining the set of alternative contextual
relationships which affect friendship patterns of the poor is as
patent as the class-linked attributes we investigated in the preceding
chapter.

Population Size and Density. Our contention that the
friendship patterns of the poor constitute an alternate system of
primary participation (in that the poor are more responsive to
neighborhood contexts unrelated to socioeconomic standing while
the solvent are more responsive to neighborhood contexts which
are class linked) now encounters an exception which proves the
rule. The size of the neighborhood population, on the face of it, has
little to do with socioeconomic rank. Yet the isolation of poor old
people is unaffected by neighborhood size, while the proportion of
isolates among solvent old people decreases steadily in progressively
larger neighborhoods, from 53 per cent where less than eighty
people reside to about 30 per cent in areas where the population
totals 155 or more. Moreover, the proportion of poor old people
with local friends decreases in larger neighborhoods, and the proportion of solvent old people with local friends increases. And the
neighborhood friendship rate of the solvent changes slightly more
than does that of the poor. The friendship patterns observed here
thus resemble those produced by the economic context of the
neighborhood. The population size of the neighborhoods in our
sample is positively associated with their wealth, the correlation is
0.49, and negatively associated with aspects of the neighborhood,
such as mean age, −0.51, to which the poor are particularly
responsive. Hence, these findings are not surprising. For working
class people under sixty-five, the size of the neighborhood has no
effect on friendship patterns.

When we measure the household density of the neighborhood, identical results emerge. For the aged poor, crowded neighborhoods—that is, those with large mean household size (computed
on a household base)—are less conducive to local friendships than
are ones with smaller mean household size. For the solvent old

people, the reverse is the case. Again, this pattern can be accounted for by the positive association between household density and socio-economic characteristics of the neighborhood. And for working class people under sixty-five, there does not seem to be any clear relationship between household density and friendship patterns.

NEIGHBORHOOD SOCIAL STRUCTURE

Up to this point, we have examined neighborhood characteristics separately and with a few exceptions as if they were unrelated for the most part. But the effects of neighborhood social contexts on friendship patterns also are functions of the interrelations among the several characteristics of the total neighborhood social environment. Some of these interrelations can be predicted. For example, we know that wealthier neighborhoods are likely to be younger neighborhoods and to contain fewer Negro households, old neighborhoods are likely to have small households, and so forth. The composite social structure of each neighborhood (insofar as it can be measured by the variables considered here) consists in the joint relationships of these and other aspects of its social composition. Neighborhoods, then, may be characterized by the form these interrelations assume, and the most highly interrelated characteristics under study can be taken as composite dimensions of neighborhood social structure and applied to the analysis of friendship patterns. We turn, then, to the descriptive task: finding those neighborhood characteristics which are associated with each other.

Philadelphia neighborhood characteristics are, by and large, interrelated as one would expect in an eastern metropolis. However, some special features of Philadelphia neighborhoods deserve comment. Because Philadelphia is an old city, many of its residential buildings date from before high-rise construction was feasible or popular. And recent urban renewal and public housing efforts notwithstanding, many of the working class people sampled in this study, both poor and solvent, old and young, are owner-residents of old row houses, as was shown in Chapter One. Thus many of the poorer areas of Philadelphia, not to say the slums, do not have the population density one associates with urban ghettos of New York City, for instance. Some parts of the city which have neighborhood population densities considerably in excess of those found in the slums are populated by relatively well-to-do white-collar (and blue-collar) families living in new high-rise apartment buildings. Hence, the correlation between mean family income per annum and number of households in the neighborhood is slight—virtually non-existent. And the correlation between neighborhood wealth and neighborhood population size is positive (0.49) and not negative as we might expect were the poor and the solvent working class people studied here packed into urban areas of high-density housing capacity. And these smaller neighborhoods tend to contain older people. The correlation between the proportion of people in the neighborhood sixty-five or more and the population size of the neighborhood is −0.40.

To reveal the main elements of neighborhood social structure which order the characteristics of the 230 blocks sampled in this study, a principal-components analysis was performed. The three leading factors, which together accounted for approximately 70 per cent of the total variance, were rotated into an orthogonal structure according to the varimax criterion. These are shown in the first five neighborhood variables in Table 9. Neighborhoods high on factor I are characterized by relatively young inhabitants, larger than average households, relatively "comfortable" family incomes, and fewer than average Negro families. Conversely, blocks with low factor I scores are likely to have more Negro families, smaller households, lower incomes, and older people. This factor is by far the most prominent. It accounts for approximately 40 per cent of the total variance and approximately 60 per cent of the analyzed variance in the original matrix. It seems to define a dimension along which blocks or neighborhoods may be rated according to one stereotype of the child-rearing "comfortable working class" section of a typical eastern city.

Factor II, consisting of variables 6 and 7 in Table 9, is associated with the size-density characteristic of the neighborhoods. It is probably a function of two effects. First, geographically large blocks are likely to contain more dwelling units and hence more people. Second, variable 7 (number of people in the block)', which has a loading of 0.52 on factor I, apparently owes a significant part of its variance to the presence of some geographically large blocks with large, multidwelling apartment buildings. Thus factor II

Table 9

VARIMAX ROTATED FACTORS

Neighborhood Variable	Factor Loadings		
	I	II	III
1. Mean age	−0.91	−0.12	−0.02
2. Mean household size (household base)	0.82	−0.09	0.14
3. Proportion 65 or older	−0.81	−0.09	0.02
4. Mean income	0.77	0.13	0.28
5. Proportion Negro households	−0.73	−0.04	0.00
6. Number of households	−0.13	0.95	0.11
7. Number of people	0.52	0.80	0.02
8. Of those over 44, proportion in the labor force	−0.08	0.11	0.90
9. Proportion male	0.33	0.00	0.70
10. Proportion married	0.60	0.04	0.43
11. Of those over 44 and in the labor force, proportion blue-collar	−0.08	−0.09	0.09

seems to define a dimension which cuts across other basic dimensions and lumps together an extensive area of row houses with an area of apartment dwellers or families or both who live in (geographically) large blocks. This interpretation is supported by the fact that none of the age, race, or income variables have appreciable loadings on this factor.

Factor III is somewhat more difficult to interpret. It is composed of neighborhood variables 8, 9, and 10 (note that variable 10 has a higher loading on factor I) in Table 9. Apparently some neighborhoods contain relatively large (and relatively small) numbers of middle-aged and older men who are in the labor force. These blocks cannot be differentiated along the dimensions of either of the other two factors. Since our analysis shows that factors

II and III bear little relationship to friendship patterns when these are arrayed against factor scores, they will not be discussed further.

Factor I emphasizes the interconnections among age, family cycle, income, and race. The continuum of local areas ranges from comfortable, white, child-rearing neighborhoods to neighborhoods where family size and child-rearing functions have atrophied, where economic rewards are lower, and where the transition to racial integration is evident. The neighborhoods with high factor I scores are the environments in which the social reproduction of working-class personnel takes place. This occurs with relatively little stress, that is, under conditions of relative economic comfort and relative lack of local interracial confrontation and its probable attendant antagonisms and anxieties (recall that our working class respondents are largely homeowners)'. The term *social reproduction* implies the socialization functions of the family and of neighborhood peers in addition to the biological element and the element of physical care of the young. Socially nonreproductive neighborhoods, on the other hand, are sites of relative economic want and racial mixture, populated by those who have advanced through the reproductive years or who have grown old without having raised children. Thus, the combination of economic deprivation, social stress in the local environment, and atrophy of certain family functions is implied by the term *socially nonreproductive.*

Consider first the aged working class people, those who themselves have passed the reproductive years. Table 10 shows the contrasting effect on the local friendship relations of poor and solvent old people of the socially reproductive character of the neighborhood context. Smaller proportions of the aged poor have local friends and larger proportions of them have friends beyond the neighborhood, the more the neighborhood possesses that congeries of characteristics which has led us to term it socially reproductive. Yet just the opposite is the case for solvent old working class people. However, the differences in the proportion of isolates among the aged who live in neighborhoods with different degrees of socially reproductive characteristics are less clear cut. The isolation of the aged poor is markedly curvilinear over factor I scores. The isolation of the age solvent, although it changes over factor I scores in the opposite direction from that of the poor, nevertheless changes

Table 10

Friendship Patterns of the Poor and the Solvent, Age Sixty-Five or More, by Factor I Scores
(in percentages)[a]

	Poor				Solvent			
	Factor I Scores							
Friendship Patterns	40 or Less (N = 50)	41 to 48 (N = 47)	49 to 56 (N = 213)	57 or More (N = 59)	40 or Less (N = 21)	41 to 48 (N = 47)	49 to 56 (N = 177)	57 or More (N = 54)
Isolates	38.0	40.4	29.1	45.8	42.9	44.7	39.5	35.2
Friends beyond the neighborhood	4.0	10.6	15.0	22.0	28.6	23.4	17.5	20.4
Friends within the neighborhood	58.0	48.9	55.9	32.2	28.6	31.9	42.9	44.4
Total	100.0	100.0	100.0	100.0	100.0	100.0	100.0	100.0

[a] Percentages may not add to 100 because of rounding.

only slightly. Still, in the main, the pattern of isolation is complementary to that of local friendships. In the most socially reproductive environments there is a larger proportion of isolated poor old people and a smaller proportion of isolated solvent old people than in any other type of neighborhood.

The effects of the socially reproductive character of the neighborhood on aged working class people resemble in direction those of neighborhood wealth and related neighborhood characteristics discussed in Chapter Two. This finding is to be expected in view of the high positive loading of neighborhood wealth on factor I. Yet the responsiveness of the aged poor to the socially reproductive character of the neighborhood is greater than that of the solvent old people—in that the difference between the highest and lowest proportions of isolates (or the highest and lowest proportion of those who have local friends) is greater for the poor than for the solvent. In this latter respect, the socially reproductive context resembles family- and life-cycle contexts which are unrelated to socioeconomic rank. The joint effect on friendship patterns of a number of characteristics making up the composite social structure of neighborhoods is a combination of the influence of two kinds of social contexts which we have separated for analytic purposes.

We are now in a position to throw some light on the differential patterns of friendship in old age and their relation to neighborhood social structure. In Table 10 the only monotonic series of changes in isolation or local friendship rates associated with the increasingly socially reproductive character of the neighborhood is in the proportions of solvent old people with local friends. The reasons lie in the preceding sections of this chapter and in the chapter before it. All the elements of factor I which make for a highly socially reproductive area—high income, young age level, large household size, and lack of Negro neighbors—are associated with higher rates of local friendship for the solvent people only among the aged subjects of our study.

In all other cases, the elements which make up factor I are at cross-purposes to some degree—that is, as far as friendship patterns are concerned. For example, consider the rate of isolation from friends of the solvent old people. We saw earlier that they were less isolated when neighborhood wealth was high and Negro neighbors were lacking; but household size had no influence on their isolation, and neighborhood age structure had little connection with the isolation of the old solvent wives (and the relationship between age and isolation was curvilinear for the others moreover). So only two of the components of factor I have a clear unidirectional association with the isolation of all solvent old people.

Or consider the aged poor. High income, young age level, and large household size each increase old poor people's isolation and decrease their local friendship rate. But a lack of Negro neighbors, which also is characteristic of the most socially reproductive neighborhoods, has the opposite effect. Doubtless, this change contributes to the lack of monotonicity in local friendship and isolation rates observed in Table 10 for the aged poor.

The significance of poverty and solvency for aged working class people, then, lies in the connection between their level of income and the elements of neighborhood structure which, combined, characterize the socially reproductive environment. The solvent old people, by virtue of their economic standing, are able to override the apparent differences in age and in family and life cycles which distinguish them from at least some of their neighbors with like degree of wealth. But poverty, in isolating the poor from neighbors of higher economic standing, also estranges them from the younger, child-rearing residents of the local area. Income differences and family- and life-cycle differences combine to erect a barrier to neighborhood affiliation which is difficult to surmount. Even the steadily increasing proportion of the aged poor who maintain local friendships outside their neighborhoods as the socially reproductive character of the area becomes more marked does not prevent their isolation from friends from rising to its high point in the neighborhoods with the highest scores on factor I, as a glance at Table 10 reveals.

However, the closer in age working class people are to the reproductive years, the less we would expect that the income differences among them would bear upon friendship relations in a differential way. Thus, there are only slight differences in the proportions of the poor and the solvent middle aged who have local friends in either socially reproductive or socially nonreproductive neighborhoods. Some of the directionality we noted above when we were considering the aged remains, it is true. Among the working class people between fifty-five and sixty-four, smaller proportions of the poor have local friends the more the neighborhood is socially reproductive, and (with the exception of the most nonreproductive areas) the opposite is the case for the solvent. But the strong differential impact of type of neighborhood on local friendships has evaporated. Approximately the same picture emerges when we consider the isolation of the poor and the solvent from friends. Only in the most socially reproductive neighborhoods is there a considerable difference between proportions of the poor (one-half) and of the solvent (one-third) who are isolated. And there is a substantial rise in the proportion of the poor who are isolated as the neighborhood becomes more socially reproductive. But the trend is upward for the solvent at this age level too.

If we consider the youngest of our respondents, those who are fifty-four and less, the differences between the poor and the solvent have virtually disappeared, and the impact of the reproductive character of the neighborhood has dwindled almost to the vanishing point.

OTHER FACTORS AND SOCIAL ISOLATION

The analysis of this and the preceding chapter has stressed the relation between neighborhood structural contexts and working class friendship patterns. Since it was couched in terms of what is essentially one set of independent variables, other factors also may contribute to the observed variation on the dependent variable side. Theoretical and common sense grounds justify examining the relevance of selected additional variables to social isolation or the lack of it.

Those who are isolated from friends may differ from non-isolates in the number of years they have lived at their present address or in the number of times they have moved from one neighborhood to another in Philadelphia. Those who have lived longer in one place may be more likely to have friends there, or, home ownership may influence the degree to which a person involves himself with others in the area. Neither of these hypotheses appears to be true, however. We find no differences whatsoever between isolates and nonisolates in the proportions among them who have lived at their present address for less than a year, between one and two years, three and five, six and ten, eleven and twenty, or twenty-one or more years. We find no differences between isolates and non-isolates in the number of times they have moved from one neighborhood to another. And there are no differences between isolates and nonisolates according to whether they own their homes, are paying off a mortgage, are renting a house, are renting an apartment, or are being supported in a house or apartment by relatives.

Perhaps the loss of friends is more closely related to isolation than to the length of local residence. At any given time, a person may be isolated because a friend has died or has moved and may not be replaced easily. That is, isolation may be a function of the attrition of a circle of acquaintances by mortality or mobility. Again, the evidence fails to bear out these suppositions. We find that 67 per cent of the isolates and 60 per cent of the nonisolates have lost no friends through death during the past five years. And virtually identical proportions of isolates and nonisolates have lost one, two, three, four, or five or more friends during that period. Similarly, the proportions of isolates and nonisolates who have lost friends because they have moved away are nearly identical.

However, the number of friends lost by death or geographical mobility may be irrelevant in itself and the ability to make up such losses by forming new friendships or activating dormant relations with those who once were friends may be what distinguishes a person who remains integrated into a circle of friendly affiliation from one who becomes isolated. Accordingly, we asked those who had lost friends through death or mobility during the past five years whether, for each lost friend, they found another to help make up that loss. Once more the evidence denies the possibility. Among isolates and nonisolates who lost a friend through death, identical proportions were unable to replace friends. And this finding remains true when we control for the number of friends who have died. Exactly the same may be said of isolates and nonisolates whose friends have moved away.

Of factors less directly connected with friends, none seem to be related to isolation or the lack of it. Neither educational level, religion, ethnic origin, or whether the respondent is an immigrant or first, second, or third generation citizen differentiates the isolates from the nonisolates. Nothing about the employment history of the breadwinners or former breadwinners in our sample is related to isolation. Isolates and nonisolates are no different from each other with respect to whether they have ever been unemployed, the time at which they were unemployed, or the number of periods of unemployment they have experienced. Regularity of working hours appears to be only a negligible factor. Of those in the labor force during 1960 to 1964, we found 62 per cent of the nonisolates had regular working hours compared to 53 per cent of the isolates. Indexes of occupational change and income change over a lifetime of work also fail to distinguish between isolates and nonisolates. Condition of health, as measured by a perceived disease index, also makes no difference.

However, for one small segment of our sample, there was a substantial difference between isolates and nonisolates in terms of perceived social mobility. As we mentioned in Chapter One, we asked the respondents what class they placed themselves in now and then followed with a series of questions concerning what classes they thought they had moved from and into during their lives. These responses were coded into categories indicating perceived upward or downward social mobility. Only ninety of the isolates and 205 of the nonisolates saw themselves as having moved at all—representing 17 and 20 per cent, respectively, of all those without and with friends. But among this small portion of the respondents who perceived themselves as having been mobile, more of the isolates (66 per cent) than of the nonisolates (49 per cent) thought they had moved downward. However, the number of cases involved here is too small to have a significant bearing on the preceding analysis.

CONCLUSION

In this chapter we have continued our examination of the influence of neighborhood structural contexts on patterns of friendship. After having explored, in the preceding chapter, the way class-linked neighborhood structural contexts differentially affect the friendship patterns of poor and solvent working class people, we turned our attention to a set of structural contexts which are not on the face of it related to the socioeconomic rank of neighborhood residents. These contexts refer instead to broadly defined stages of the family cycle and the life cycle insofar as they are measured by the marital status and by the age of neighborhood residents. In assessing the impact of family- and life-cycle contexts on patterns of friendship in the working class, we retained for purposes of this analysis the distinction between poor and solvent respondents. Since we had found in investigating class-linked contexts that the strength and direction of the effect of neighborhood composition on friendship patterns differed for poor and solvent, we sought to determine whether family- and life-cycle contexts also had similarly differential functions with respect to friendship and isolation from friends.

We did discover that family- and life-cycle contexts differentially affect poor and solvent working class people's friendship patterns. But the nature of this differential impact indicates an alternative system of neighborhood primary social participation for the poor. Whereas it was demonstrated in Chapter Two that poor working class people, and mainly the aged males among them, are less responsive than the solvent to class-linked contexts (and to the extent that the poor were affected by class-linked contexts they were isolated by those contextual conditions which promote integration into local friendship relations for the solvent) now in this chapter it was shown that poor working class people are highly responsive to family- and life-cycle contexts. But the solvent people's friendship relations remain virtually unaffected by such contexts. Where the neighborhood is a source of supply of people who have reached relatively advanced family- and life-cycle stages, the poor are proportionately less isolated and more integrated into neighborhood friendships than where neighbors are predominantly young and at early family-cycle stages. Thus the dynamics of the family- and life-cycle context in patterning working class friendship relations is markedly different from what we observed when we considered class-linked contexts. We are not dealing here with a set of contextual effects which bear more heavily on the poor than on the solvent. The solvent working class people sampled in this study simply do not respond in terms of friendship relations to this system of neighborhood structural contexts. Had the solvent respondents been strongly affected by family- and life-cycle contexts and the poor less so, then it might have been possible to conceive of the system of primary participation of the poor as a variant of the working class mode. The poor could have been thought of as victims of deprivation and therefore somehow less sensitive to more conventional forms of social influence. Or any number of interpretations based essentially on the underdog model could have been adduced. However, the data indicate a genuinely alternative set of contextual influences on the friendship relations of the poor in which their solvent peers do not apparently participate.

An additional increment of weight is lent this interpretation by the fact that these contextual effects in many cases extend to poor women and to men and women below sixty-five. If the impact of social class is felt, through neighborhood structural context, on the friendship relations of old males chiefly, then the independence of family- and life-cycle influences on friendship is further supported by evidence of its wider scope.

The burden of evidence of this chapter, when juxtaposed with the findings of the preceding chapter, also points to a more general conclusion. One of the ways in which the social integration of people at disparate levels within the working class is accomplished is through the articulation of alternative structural contexts of primary participation. Structural contexts appear in this sense to be selective mechanisms of social integration and social isolation. Thus taxonomic efforts to describe the general social condition of the aged, the poor, the lower working class, and combinations thereof, or any social category (no matter how labeled) believed to be malintegrated into the larger society by the use of such descriptors as alienated, isolated, and disengaged may be assisted by the following prescription, which appears to result from the analysis of this and the preceding chapters: Malintegration categories of social analysis can be filled only when alternative, selective mechanisms of social integration are absent.

This chapter concluded with a factor-analytic demonstration that the joint influence of class-linked and family- and life-cycle structural contexts on the friendship patterns of our working class respondents was mixed. Factors descriptive of the composite neighborhood structural context were loaded to include elements of both systems which operate at cross-purposes in determining rates of local friendship and isolation from friends of poor and solvent people. In this way, a multivariate technique describing a composite social entity, the structure of the neighborhood, masked functions previously discerned by analysis of the separate elements of local social structure as they differentially affected population subgroups within the neighborhood.

CHAPTER **4**

Age Status Homophily and Heterophily

Nor is my enjoyment confined to gatherings with my own age fellows, of whom very few are still alive, but I find it also with men of your generation.

CICERO
On Old Age

n the preceding chapters, we dealt with working class isolation from friends and also with the integration of working class people into local friendship networks from the standpoint of the opportunities for social interaction supplied or denied members of our sample by the social composition of their neighborhoods. In so doing, we did not explore directly the precise nature of the friendship pairs formed under different contextual conditions. We went so far as to surmise that the supply of status-similars was in some manner involved in the contextual determination of friendship and isolation rates. But we stopped short of inferring that those friendships which did exist in areas well supplied with status-similars were in fact made up of status-similars. Status homophily may indeed be the precise mechanism by which friendships are formed in contextually consonant neighborhoods, and potential status heterophily may well be the precise condition which prevents pairing in contextually dissonant neighborhoods and thereby determines isolation rates. But no evidence was adduced to support directly either surmise about mechanisms. Our argument in the preceding chapters did not require it. There our goal was to elucidate contextual relationships, and our main emphasis was on accounting for the lack of friendship relations. We did not set out to describe the character of friendships formed or to emphasize rates of friendship relations except insofar as they contributed to a picture of the problem of isolation. Furthermore, in a rigorously logical sense, the problem of social isolation from friends would not be illuminated directly by examining the homophilous or heterophilous relationships of the sample members because the design of this study is nonexperimental. However, in spite of this prior focus, several other good and sufficient reasons exist for examining, relatively briefly, some aspects of homophily and heterophily among our working class respondents.

First, anything we can learn about the heterogeneity or homogeneity of working class social relations is likely to throw some light, if only inferentially, on larger questions about the nature of the separation of the working class from the larger society in a sense heretofore unmentioned but nevertheless part of any broad view of the problem of working class social isolation. It has been known for some time, for instance, that at every socioeconomic level, class homophily is the modal pattern of informal social relationships in adolescence and in adulthood. Cross-class cliques and friendships occur of course, but the presumption has been that they occur with less frequency at the lowest levels of the class hierarchy. From the time of Marx and Weber up through the present, researchers have utilized these observations as the basis of theories specifying how working class consciousness and working class communal action may come about or have employed them as indicators of a general lack of integration of the working class into the larger society. However, these large considerations concerning the integration of the working class, as a specific segment of the socioeconomic hierarchy, into the society as a whole may depend on criteria other than or additional to those which are class linked. If class homophily predominates in the working class to a greater extent than elsewhere, leading to the conclusion that working class systems of informal social relations harden class boundaries because they minimize interclass communication and understanding, we are bound to ask whether there are other social divisions across which interaction occurs in the working class before we accept a thesis which tends to equate class discontinuities with general social separateness. Perhaps then the question of the lack of integration of the working class into the larger society should be reformulated so that we may inquire whether working class integration is accomplished through informal social relationships which span divisions of the society other than class. Since this study does not examine the middle class, we cannot identify cross-cutting areas of informal social participation which are unique to the working class. But later in this chapter, we indicate for the working class alone whether heterophily occurs along a non-class–linked dimension of social relations. Others then may make the cross-class comparison more efficiently.

A second reason for examining homophily and heterophily among our working class respondents is related to the foregoing reason, yet distinguishable from it. It refers to the isolation of the working class but in a different sense. The integration of working class people into the larger society through interaction spanning social boundaries is not the issue, as it was above. Here, by isolation we mean low frequency of interaction, not lack of diversity among parties to interaction. The rates of social participation in informal social relations may be lower in the working class than in the middle class. However, the argument could be made that there is a relationship between low rates of interaction and the homogeneity of participants. That is, if normative precepts restrict participation in informal relations to those who are similar, the choice is narrowed, and the total rate of interaction is less than it might be were a diversity of partners tolerated—or less than the rate which exists elsewhere in the society where dissimilar people commonly interact. This argument or a variant of it often is implicit in cross-class comparisons of rates of interaction. Again, our study design does not include middle class respondents, so we cannot contribute to this issue conclusively. But some clarification can be introduced simply by examining some aspects of similarity and dissimilarity of social characteristics among friends within the working class. The argument rests on the assumption that the role sets of working class people are homophilous (while those of middle class people are less so or are predominantly heterophilous). Any evidence of marked heterophily on some reasonable social characteristic in working class role sets would tend to undermine this argument. In such a situation, one would then focus attention on other structural differences in the role sets of middle and working class people in future research.

But in the light of the preceding chapters, we must also consider the impact of the neighborhood structural context in order to determine whether homophilous role sets occur in contextually dissonant as well as in contextually consonant environments. The maintenance of homophilous role sets in contextually dissonant environments in the working class may constitute strong evidence for the existence of normative working class prescriptions which keep interaction rates below what they might be were interaction with dissimilars permitted, although homophily in the face of contextual consonance may indicate nothing more than lack of opportunity to interact with dissimilars. On the other hand, heterophilous working class role sets maintained in contextually consonant environments would be presumptive evidence that working class norms

exist which contradict the assumption that similarity of role partners is the rule. In this case, one would have the option of questioning whether in fact working class interaction rates are relatively low
or of looking elsewhere for the source of low interaction rates. And
heterophilous working class role sets maintained in contextually
dissonant environments parallel the situation where homophily is
prevalent in contextually consonant environments: Lack of opportunity to interact with similars rather than normative prescription is
the most likely determinant of the interaction which will occur.

Thus an examination of homophily and heterophily in this
working class sample, in addition to having some substantive
benefits in elucidating whether putative low rates of interaction
stem from constraints to affiliate with similars, also has implications for theory. From the discussion above, there is a necessary
connection between role set (homophily) theory and structural
context theory. One is the reciprocal of the other. Strong contextual
effects tend to minimize the normative and other (structural)
factors which influence the composition of the role set; strong
tendencies toward homophily or heterophily of a normative or other
(structural) nature tend to minimize contextual effects. This is a
formal statement of relationship between theory fragments. It says
nothing about the direction of contextual or other effects with
respect to any given dependent variable which may be under
investigation.

Finally, a third reason for examining homophily and heterophily among our working class respondents concerns their age. The
older segment of the working class, especially those over sixty-five,
may be considered a critical test group. If working class people are
not fully integrated into the larger society and if this nonintegration
is reflected in the homophily of their social relationships, then the
aged working class may well display the strongest tendency to affiliate with persons of similar social characteristics. They are the least
socially mobile, lowered income restricts their motility, and retirement removes a potential source of contact with others who may
differ from them in some respects. In general, their age conspires
to limit their social life to a narrower range than they might have
experienced previously. Likewise, if working class people interact
less frequently than others because role sets are restricted to similars

within the working class, then the aged remain, for the same reasons as given above, a strategic social category for investigation.

In sum, the homophily of the role sets of working class people emerges from this discussion as a datum of prime importance. It has resonance for several arguments concerning the integration of the working class into the larger society. When combined with data on contextual consonance, it is illustrative of a connection between two branches of theory. And by virtue of their age, the old working class people represent one of the best possible social sites at which to find homophilous interactions; if they are prevalent anywhere in the working class, it is likely to be among the aged.

We have chosen to investigate age status homophily in part because of the interesting effects of neighborhoods of increasing mean age on solvent old working class people. These effects, which we commented upon in Chapter Three, tended to raise at least some doubt about the principle that neighborhood contextual consonance integrates residents into local friendship networks. But this choice of age status homophily is also made in view of gerontological theories about the nature of the aged as a special category in American society. Barron (1961)˙ puts forth the idea that the aged constitute a quasiminority group within the larger society. Those who have reached old age, he contends, have a consciousness of kind as a reaction to discrimination by younger adults, and this consciousness may be a precondition for joint action—for example, political action—in the future on the basis of their age status. Rose (1965)˙ advances the notion of the emerging subculture of the aging. This view presumes a set of common norms and values which arise essentially from a combination of position in the life cycle and the reaction of the majority culture to the status of old age. Both of these orientations toward the nature of old age in our society go beyond conceiving of old age as a period of withdrawal. They add positive elements of cohesion of the aged with respect to awareness of a common condition and possession of a distinctive common culture. From the premise that such outlooks on the part of the aged segments of our population cannot exist without a basis in interaction among those who share the condition of old age, it would seem particularly appropriate to focus on age status homophily.

To begin, we assess the level of age status homophily under conditions of neighborhood age contextual consonance and dissonance. The meaning of data about the homophilous or heterophilous character of social relations in unclear until some account can be taken of how great an opportunity is afforded an individual for either kind of affiliation. Moreover, as we have indicated, the question of contextual effects on homophily and heterophily has an independent interest. Possibly the mechanism of affiliation as well as the rate of affiliation are functions of neighborhood structural context. The critical point of inquiry, then, concerns the impact of age structural context on age status homophily.

This impact involves essentially the entire role set of friends, those who live outside as well as within the area defined by the contextual variable. Although the neighborhood is the chief locus of friendship (most respondents with friends have at least one in the neighborhood), the role played by the local age context in friendship in general involves the net balance of age status homophily in the complete circle of friends. The ultimate consequence of living among many or few age peers for the homophily or heterophily in the entire role set of friends may be concealed by confining the analysis to neighborhood friends. Given the small numbers of friends possessed by each respondent, the proportion of people with age peer affiliations may be shifted radically by adding to the analysis even one friend who lives outside the neighborhood. Moreover, if, for instance, local friendships are sustained among age-similars and nonlocal friendships among age-dissimilars, the effect on friendship in general of living among people of a given age level is systematically distorted unless friends are considered in the aggregate. At least in theory, a person can compensate for lack of friends near at hand by seeking affiliation elsewhere. Thus the focus here is on the proportion of working class people, of varying ages, who have age-similars or age-dissimilars among all their friends and the variations in these proportions which occur under different conditions of neighborhood age structure.

AGE HOMOPHILOUS ROLE SETS

The effect of neighborhood age structure (as measured by the mean age of the neighborhood population) on age status homophily is shown in Table 11, which indicates the proportion of respondents with some age status homophily in their total set of friendly affiliations as it varies by neighborhood age structure. The figures in parentheses to the right of each cell are the total number of respondents of a given age who live in neighborhoods of a particular mean age. Table 11 contains the entire number of non-isolated persons, 1,051, in the sample. The criterion—one friend who is an age peer—by which a respondent may qualify as having an element of homophily in his role set is, to say the least, partial and permissive. And the definition of who is an age peer is broad. The chances for a member of this working class sample to be categorized as maintaining age homophilous friendships could hardly be increased. Yet the clear import of Table 11 is that even under these most relaxed of criteria age status homophily is scarcely a ubiquitous phenomenon. In six of the twelve cells of the table, age homophilous role sets fail to characterize as many as half of the respondents. Regardless of the influence of the neighborhood structural context, to which we shall return shortly, age status homophily is considerably less than the predominating form of affiliation in these working class role sets.

The implications of the facts that age homophilous role sets do not clearly predominate and that age heterophily exists in substantial measure among our working class respondents are far-reaching. Whether or not working class friendships are mainly confined to class peers, they indubitably cut across age boundaries. Therefore, a structural basis seems to exist in the system of age grading for the integration of working class people into the larger society. Their friendships span age categories of at least ten years (since although our respondents are classified by age intervals, their friends who do not fall within these same intervals of age are counted as members of the respondents' heterophilous role sets no matter how much younger or older than the respondents such friends may be)'. Whatever discontinuities may exist in interclass friendship relations, we cannot add to them on the basis of age. In addition, if rates of informal social interaction in the working class are indeed lower than elsewhere, this is not because of normative restrictions on role set heterogeneity based on age. On the average, respondents possess roughly similar amounts of role set homophily no matter what their

Table 11

WORKING CLASS PEOPLE OF VARYING AGE LEVELS WITH AT LEAST ONE FRIEND WHO IS AN AGE PEER BY MEAN AGE OF NEIGHBORS

Mean Age of Neighbors	Respondent's Age							
	75 or More		65 to 74		55 to 64		54 or Less	
	Per Cent	N	Per Cent	N	Per Cent	N	Per Cent	N
0 to 34	24.1	(29)	43.1	(137)	49.2	(132)	57.4	(176)
35 to 44	18.4	(38)	54.1	(133)	42.5	(120)	55.3	(132)
45 or more	33.3	(24)	72.1	(61)	52.9	(51)	66.7	(18)

age level, and this amount is far from overwhelming. The oldest people, those between seventy-five and seventy-nine, are an exception. However, they have much less, not much more, role set homophily than do the younger working class people.

But perhaps the most compelling implications of the finding that a substantial amount of age heterophily exists among our respondents concern those theories which posit among older people some social cohesion which stems from their age and from the evaluation placed on old age in the American culture. The data reported in Table 11 do not lend much support to these formulations, which seem to depend heavily on positive elements such as characteristics of interaction rather than on negative ones such as rates of isolation. On a straightforward interpretation, they seem to require some preponderance of interaction among those of a common age level. But this preponderance does not obtain. Or at the very least, they seem to require a preponderance of age status homophily among those over sixty-five. Again, this is not what we find. No clear difference in proportions, averaged over all neighborhoods, of those over and under sixty-five with respect to age status homophily can be seen in Table 11. And the one large discrepancy, the lower level of homophily among the very oldest respondents, goes in the opposite direction from that which such theories require. And all of this occurs in that area of the society, the lower levels of the working class, where we would predict the best chances of finding such homophilous patterns of social relationships.

However, it may well be that as broadly as we have defined the boundaries of the age range within which we term a friend an age peer, we have still not considered the age grading system fairly. Perhaps in a youth-oriented society the issue is more fairly posed as one involving the direction of the age difference rather than the sheer fact of age difference. That is, it may well be that the critical fact about heterophily is that the younger people have older friends and that the aged have younger friends. We shall examine data bearing on this issue shortly. But before doing so, let us return to Table 11—this time to assess what, if any, effect on homophily is attributable to the neighborhood age context.

Although Table 11 does not show overwhelming amounts

of age status homophily among the members of the sample, there are some indications that age contextual consonance, to a limited extent, does promote age status homophily at certain age levels. Thus, if we look at the relatively small proportions of working class people seventy-five or more with age peers for friends, we can grant that doubtless this finding reflects the lack of availability of age peers in the late years because of mortality. But there is a very small increase with age of neighbors in the proportion of these very old people who have age homophilous relations. Yet it is no greater than the increase in homophily among the youngest people in the youngest as opposed to the oldest neighborhoods.

The most striking effect of neighborhood age structure on the age homophilous nature of working class pairing occurs for people between sixty-five and seventy-four. We noted in Chapter Three that at this age level, but not younger, the neighborhood age structure influences the degree of isolation from friends and the extent to which local friendships are maintained. We now see that the mechanism by which this neighborhood contextual effect occurs is the increase in age status homophily beyond what obtains for younger people living in neighborhoods of similar age structure.[1] But this is a minor trend in the over-all picture represented by Table 11 because so few of the people in this age range live in the oldest, most contextually consonant, neighborhoods.

The increased homophily of these older people, from sixty-five to seventy-four, in neighborhoods of greater contextual consonance and the other slightly increased homophily in the more age consonant neighborhoods support the interpretation we put on the generally modest levels of homophily which characterize the sample as a whole. Such homophily as we do find does not indicate a distinctive set of working class prescriptions to affiliate with similars and to avoid dissimilars but is attributable to increased opportunity for interaction with others of like age. Conversely, if we focus on the neighborhoods which are most clearly dissonant age contexts

[1] As was noted in the preceding chapter, the concentration of old people in a neighborhood, e.g., the proportion over sixty-five, so rarely reaches 40 per cent that exceedingly few respondents live in such areas. Hence it is highly unlikely that the effect of neighborhood age structure on age homophily, reported in Table 11, is merely a statistical artifact.

for our respondents, those where the mean age of the population
is lowest, we observe that the proportion of homophilous affiliations
is progressively increased the younger the respondent. Thus, reading
Table 11 across the columns, we note the monotonicity of the
decline, with increasing age, of the proportion of working class
people in the youngest neighborhoods who have age homophilous
relations. This pattern of decline in homophily is nowhere else so
strong as in the youthful localities, which are the modal residential
areas of those of our working class respondents with friends. The
maintenance of proportionately fewer age homophilous ties by
successively older cohorts of working class people in youthful
neighborhoods contrasts with the comparatively stable level of age
homophilous friendships maintained by people in neighborhoods
with older residents—excepting, of course, the steep decline in age
homophily occurring in all neighborhoods for respondents seventy-
five or older. Thus, homophily is a contextual, not a normative
phenomenon.

In a neighborhood with young residents, then, the older a
person is, the less his circle of friends consists of age peers. And for
the brief span between sixty-five and seventy-four, living in a
neighborhood with older people radically increases the chances for
age homophilous relations in the working class before the natural
attrition of peers takes its toll. Beyond this, the incidence of age
status homophily hovers somewhat above or below 50 per cent
for the working class people under consideration depending either
on their age or on the age structure of the neighborhood.

AGE HETEROPHILOUS ROLE SETS

As we have just seen, by no means all working class friendship pairs are composed of age peers. But are age heterophilous
relations maintained with predominantly older or younger people?
And what is the effect of neighborhood age structure on each form
of heterophily? As we mentioned above, the social significance of
the term *homophily* may not reside exclusively in a particular
numerically defined similarity in age among friends. And friendships which cross relatively narrowly defined age boundaries may
not be heterophilous in more than name. A more meaningful conception of age difference may encompass all older or all younger

friends without regard to the size of the span of years between them. Or a more meaningful distinction between friends of different ages may be whether the affiliation links people on either side of sixty-five. By considering the differences among friends more broadly than by ten-year intervals, we may elucidate the significance of the considerable amount of heterophilous interaction which we know occurs in this working class sample, as well as that of the more narrowly defined homophilies. For example, a certain configuration of age heterophily may lead us to suspect that restrictive norms concerning friendship do exist in spite of the lack of totally age homophilous role sets. If our respondents viewed only old age as being a "different" age from their own, we might find that relatively few friendship pairs were constituted so that our respondents were the younger partner and that this pattern occurred for respondents of all ages and in neighborhoods with predominantly old as well as with predominantly young residents. Such evidence would necessitate modification of the interpretation of the findings on age homophily. If on the contrary our respondents' heterophilous role sets included friends older than themselves, especially older friends who were past sixty-five, and if the proportion of such friendships increased the more aged people were available in the neighborhood, this finding would support strongly the interpretation given in the preceding section of this chapter. Namely, the lack of completely or largely homophilous role sets is genuinely indicative of integration across age boundaries in the working class.

Table 12 arrays by mean age of neighbors the proportion of friendships of working class people of various ages in which the respondent's friend is older. The proportion of age heterophilous relations here is uniformly low compared with the homophilous pairings in Table 11. However, friendships with older people are far from absent. And neighborhood age structure does influence the rate of heterophilous pairing. These contextual effects are strongest among the two younger cohorts, those fifty-four or less and those fifty-five to sixty-four. The proportion of their friendships with people older than themselves increases markedly when their neighbors are older. But there is no such strong tendency for greatly increased pairing with older friends among the older respondents.

Table 12

WORKING CLASS PEOPLE OF VARYING AGE LEVELS WITH OLDER FRIENDS BY MEAN AGE OF NEIGHBORS

Mean Age of Neighbors	Respondent's Age					
	65 to 74		55 to 64		54 or Less	
	Per Cent	N	Per Cent	N	Per Cent	N
0 to 34	16.1	(137)	17.4	(132)	12.1	(176)
35 to 44	12.0	(133)	21.7	(120)	15.2	(132)
45 or more	21.3	(61)	41.4	(51)	33.3	(18)

Table 12 then tends to support the interpretation we placed on the extent of age homophily revealed in Table 11. Friendships of our respondents occur with older people. And the conventionally defined boundary marking the onset of old age, sixty-five years, is crossed as frequently as not in the friendships of members of our sample younger than sixty-five. In Table 12, all the friendships with people older than themselves of respondents between fifty-five and sixty-four are by definition with people over sixty-five. For these respondents, the proportion with friends over sixty-five is the modal proportion in every type of neighborhood, young or old. In addition, the impact of a plentiful supply of older people in the neighborhood is strongest for these respondents, which indicates that they apparently feel no strong restriction on maintaining friendships with older people.

By reading across the columns of Table 12, we may gauge the effects of the age of the respondent on his propensity to form friendships with older people within neighborhoods of similar age structure. In the localities with the youngest people, the age of the respondent scarcely matters: Between 12 and 17 per cent of the friendships of working class people of all age levels consist of older friends in these neighborhoods. In the oldest neighborhoods however, the proportion of older friendships drops off steeply after sixty-five. We saw, in Table 11, that the working class people of this age level, sixty-five to seventy-four, who live in neighborhoods with old residents have the largest proportion of homophilous relationships, which partly accounts for the postretirement drop. Another factor involved here is the very high proportion of old friends built up in the years immediately preceding sixty-five by people living in these oldest neighborhoods. As we shall see shortly, this is in some measure a function of poverty. Thus, although in general living in the older neighborhoods tends to increase the chance that working class people of any age will form friendships with older friends, still, those of our respondents who are past sixty-five and who live in neighborhoods with old people fall off in the rate at which they make older friends much more sharply than do their counterparts in neighborhoods with younger people.

But younger friends are not necessarily more frequently found in neighborhoods with younger people. Both the oldest (seventy-five or more) and the youngest (fifty-five to sixty-four)' cohorts of working class people have smaller proportions of friendships with young people in these neighborhoods than in neighborhoods with old residents, which is the opposite of what we might expect if contextual consonance governed the age of friends as well as isolation from friends. Having younger friends is associated with living in a young neighborhood chiefly for the sixty-five to seventy-four age group. But in all cases, the differences are moderate.

Further examination of the data indicates that the balance of age heterophilous pairs weighs definitely toward the younger side. But we can say this for the middle two age cohorts merely since these are the only ones which permit a direct comparison. (The definition of older and younger friends adopted here rules out the possibilities that people seventy-five or older can have "older" friends and that people fifty-four or younger can have "younger" friends.)

In sum, we cannot say that there are barriers to affiliation with the aged for people who are not old themselves or that there is strong partiality for friendship formation with people younger than our respondents. People not yet sixty-five are willing in fairly substantial numbers to cross the conventionally defined line demarcating old age when old people are available in sufficient numbers. But people over sixty-five do not show so substantial an increase in the rate of friendships with younger people in neighborhoods with the youngest as compared with those with the oldest people. And although on balance there appear to be more friendships with younger than with older people in the sample as a whole, still a comparison which juxtaposes the rate of friendship with older people in localities with the oldest people with that of friendship with younger people in localities with the youngest people shows very little difference. In those areas in which the possibility for friendships with older and younger persons is greatest, the net result of structured opportunity and other unmeasured factors which may tip the rate of affiliation in one or the other direction is virtual equalization of the two forms of age heterophilous patterns. Integration into the larger society occurs along the age hierarchy in the working class through the mechanism of age heterogeneous role sets; and it occurs by tying middle-aged and old working class people into primary social relations in about equal measure with persons older and younger than themselves, given favorable contextual conditions. Thus, theories about the malintegration of the working class do not apply to social differentiation by age, and theories concerning subcultural or minority group standing of the older age cohorts of the population lack a basis in the interaction patterns of this segment of the working class.

ROLE OF POVERTY

Since we have found, in Chapter Three, that the poor are more responsive than the solvent to the age structure of the neighborhood (at least insofar as isolation from or integration into friendship networks is concerned) and since we have just seen the nature of the impact of neighborhood age structure on age status homophily in the entire role set of friends for the sample as a whole, we now raise the question of the role of poverty in age homophily. A small case base prevents us from dealing with the joint influence of poverty and age of neighbors on homophily. But we can approach the question indirectly by considering poverty and solvency apart from the neighborhood context and then attempt to make some inferences about the relative importance of the socioeconomic condition of the respondents and the age structure of the neighborhood.

The point requiring elucidation is the nature of the alternative mode of primary participation which, as we have seen, characterizes poor working class people. Does the responsiveness of the poor to family- and life-cycle contexts itself represent a lack of integration on the basis of age, in the sense that their interaction is confined to age peers more than that of the solvent? Age contextual consonance may promote the local friendships of the poor. But does it circumscribe them within a narrow age range? Perhaps, the effect of poverty is manifestly restrictive along an age dimension rather than along a class dimension.

In only one age cohort do the poor and solvent differ in the degree to which they have age homophilous relations. This is shown in Table 13. Among respondents fifty-five to sixty-four, proportionately more poor than solvent people have age peers as friends. In every other age cohort, there is no difference between the poor

Table 13

POOR AND SOLVENT WORKING CLASS PEOPLE BY AGE BY NUMBER OF FRIENDS AGE FIFTY-FIVE TO SIXTY-FOUR
(in percentages)[a]

Number of Friends 55 to 64	Respondent's Age					
	Poor			Solvent		
	65 or More (N = 242)	55 to 64 (N = 76)	54 or Less (N = 48)	65 or More (N = 180)	55 to 64 (N = 227)	54 or Less (N = 278)
0	60.7	42.1	54.2	61.7	56.4	78.1
1	27.7	40.8	37.5	26.7	27.3	17.3
2	7.9	10.5	8.2	8.9	10.1	3.2
3 or more	3.7	6.6	—	2.8	6.1	1.5
Total	100.0	100.0	100.0	100.0	100.0	100.0

[a] Percentages may not add to 100 because of rounding.

and the solvent in age status homophily. (These data are not presented.) The greater degree of age homophily of the poor in this age cohort is accounted for by the larger proportion of the impoverished having out of their entire circle of acquaintances only one age peer as a friend. The role set of friends of the poor is not more saturated with age peers, in the sense that the number of homophilous pairs formed by a poor individual is greater than for a solvent individual. Instead there is a larger proportion of people with one and only one homophilous role partner among the poor. Table 13 reveals another difference between the poor and solvent. Among the poor who are fifty-four or less, the amount of heterophily of the sort constituted by having older friends, that is, friends fifty-five to sixty-four, is greater than among the solvent.

In general then, the evidence on the relation between poverty and age homophily is inconclusive but suggestive nevertheless. The evidence indicates that the role of economic standing in age homophilous pairing is with one exception nonexistent. But the exception conforms to a characteristic picture of the nature of the social life of the poor: The affiliations of the poor contain less variety than do those of the solvent.

If the poor are conceived of as less venturesome than those more secure, if they are thought of as less willing to incur the risks and rebuffs inherent in associations with people different from themselves, then we would expect that their friendships would be characterized by a relative preponderance of similars. And we would expect this, moreover, on the general theorem that those who stand low in a hierarchy have a greater homogeneity in their role sets than do those who stand higher. That this should be true with respect to age homophily, in the particular years which represent the last decade of working life, we would tentatively (and admittedly without a shred of evidence at this point) ascribe to the realization on the part of the poor that if economic success has not come by now, it is unlikely ever to come. In the years following retirement, the mechanisms of contextual consonance and dissonance, described in Chapters Two and Three, may govern friendship relations, although what differential bearing they may have on age homophily for the poor and the solvent is an unexamined issue. But in the absence of such mechanisms in the decade under discussion, the protection afforded one's self-esteem by interaction with others whose chances for rising economically are as circumscribed as one's own may be considerable. Some slight support for this line of reasoning may be found in the differing patterns of affiliation of poor and solvent respondents fifty-four or less, revealed in Table 13. If these younger people are poor, a larger proportion have older friends than if they are solvent. That is, the poor more than the solvent have friends whose life chances are already fixed to a greater degree than their own. Young solvent people have little to gain by maintaining friendships with people older than themselves. Presumably they judge their economic standing to be viable still and their chances for improvement not yet foreclosed. Then, proportionately fewer of them have a stake in maintaining friendships with people whose chances are less than their own. The poor, on the other hand, may well regard their own situation with pessimism, even at fifty-four or less. Friendship with older people may represent a form of insulation from the stress of interaction with others who may yet outstrip them economically.

CONCLUSION

In this chapter, we have briefly considered the impact of the age structure of the neighborhood and the economic standing of our respondents on age status homophily. We have turned, that is, from the characterization of working class friendship networks in terms of quantity—lack of friends and having one or more friends—to a characterization of the entire role set of friends in terms of quality. The particular quality we have attempted to analyze is the variability in age of the friends of our respondents.

The analysis in this chapter has revealed again the potency of the neighborhood context: The older the neighborhood the more likely are working class people of any age to have age peers as friends; but those most likely to have age homophilous relations under the most favorable local conditions are people who are themselves old, over sixty-five.

But substantial amounts of age status heterophily were also found—heterophily which included younger as well as older friends in the role sets of our working class respondents. These friendship pairs often span the conventional dividing line between middle and old age—sixty-five years. The total evidence on homophily and heterophily of age seems to indicate considerable integration of older working class people into the larger society along this ascriptive dimension of social differentiation. In this respect, the aged as a group (within the limits of the sample) in the working class can hardly be considered a separated enclave of the society. The structural basis for assuming subcultural or quasiminority group status for the aged seems to be absent for the most part.

Restrictive informal participation along an age dimension, where it occurs, seems to be indirectly related to socioeconomic rank rather than age. Although in general there appears to be little connection between poverty and solvency and age homophily, we did find some among those fifty-five to sixty-four. Here the role sets of the poor are more homophilous than those of the solvent; and also the poor make friends, to a greater degree than the solvent, with people older than themselves. These findings, we speculate, fit best with the theorem that low standing in a hierarchy leads to homogeneous role sets more frequently than does high standing. In the case under consideration, we interpret the data as meaning that the poor have arrived at an age where they see no hope of economic improvement; therefore, they insulate themselves from people with better life chances by confining their affiliations to age peers more frequently than do the solvent. This interpretation is slightly supported by the finding that the younger poor, those fifty-four or less, tend to have older friends (that is, friends fifty-five to sixty-four) more frequently than their solvent counterparts do. The younger poor people thus maintain friends whose life chances are more fixed than their own to a greater extent than do the solvent.

CHAPTER  5

Working Class Kinship Relations

Though you have shelters and institutions,
Precarious lodgings while the rent is paid,
Subsiding basements where the rat breeds
Or sanitary dwellings with numbered doors
Or a house a little better than your neighbour's;
When the Stranger says: "What is the meaning of this
    city?"
Do you huddle close together because you love each
    other?
What will you answer? "We all dwell together
To make money from each other"? or "This is a
    community"?

                  T. S. ELIOT
                  Choruses from "The Rock"

108

Thus far we have considered friends and friendship networks in the working class. In this chapter,[1] we turn to the family, that is, to those of the respondents' primary and secondary kin who live outside his household but within the metropolitan Philadelphia area. To what extent are working class people isolated from or integrated into a kinship system? And what distinguishes those working class people who have no or little contact with kin from those who maintain more active kinship relations?

Before addressing these questions we take as broad a view as possible of some perspectives and issues in the study of the American family and the American kinship structure. Any substantial body of data about American family and kinship presented today is highly likely to become grist for the mill of one or another proponent in a series of vigorous debates over fundamental issues in family sociology and, indeed, in anthropology as well. These contested issues are so basic that almost any information about family and kinship structure or function appears to relate to some aspect of the controversy. Our concern with the way the material to be discussed later in this chapter relates to these disputes does not arise from diffidence, however. Instead, we take a position somewhat at variance with those held by the major parties to current controversy. We wish, therefore, to advocate a certain perspective toward the study of family and kinship. Furthermore, we wish to circumscribe carefully the contribution made to this point of view by the analysis of data on working class kinship which we introduce later. Our contention is that some of the terms in which the current debates are conducted make them profitless. And we are reluctant to have fruitless interpretations placed on our findings, which, in addition, from our point of view, have only certain specific relevance to the theoretical perspective toward kinship studies we wish to advance and which bear in a particular way on the question of working class isolation from kin in middle and old age.

[1] This chapter was written in collaboration with Donald Frederick Anspach.

Structural analysis of the family and of the kinship system in which it is embedded is important not because the system is an important structural unit with jural status but for theoretical reasons. Such analysis has broad implications for the operation of society and the interrelation of the kinship system with various other subsystems. (It also has, of course, practical implications with respect to welfare policies, social planning, housing, and many other vital concerns, but these are not subjects we are considering here.)

American sociologists come to the study of kinship by studying the family. In so doing, they make assumptions which affect how we study kinship. In the sociological literature, one finds a diversity of family concepts: elementary family, immediate family, conjugal family, incomplete family, empty nest family, modified extended family, and nuclear family. Often elementary, nuclear, and conjugal family are used interchangeably. The single term *nuclear family* (referring to the husband-wife-children unit) is most often used because it is believed to refer to the only major concrete unit of kinship in this society. According to Cumming and Schneider's (1961) findings, the nuclear family is culturally defined as the ideal residence group in American society.

Without a comparative focus, American sociologists took Murdock's (1949) position on the universality of the nuclear family too literally. Murdock suggests that this group serves four universal functions: economic, regulation of sexual relationships, reproduction, and socialization. From one point of view, the Murdock thesis and the tradition of research founded upon it are vague and incomplete and fail to distinguish, as Levy and Fallers (1959) point out, at least three analytical meanings of the nuclear family concept: as a concrete unit, as a particular structural type, and as an invariant set of functions.

The confounding of these separate analytic aspects has led to the implication that the size of the nuclear family contracts as members move or take meals at another house, as Lancaster (1961) notes. This implication becomes a major premise for sociologists who use the life-cycle approach to the family. For example, the empty nest family is used to refer to the household unit consisting of husband and wife, after their children have left to form their own families. However, as Lancaster (1961) recognizes, many of the functions—such as physical maintenance, socialization, and regulation of sexual relations—attributed to the entity termed the nuclear family are in fact predicated upon the regular existence of some form of concrete domestic unit, which does not have to be composed of the personnel or the bundle of roles which we label *nuclear family* today.

The thesis of the universality of the nuclear family has led to the premise that it is the minimal socializing unit of any society. Levy and Fallers (1959) suggest that although there may be a structural requisite for small kin-based domestic units for socialization, it does not follow that this unit is the nuclear family or that the nuclear family is the sole unit performing this function. In addition, characterizing the nuclear family as the minimal socializing unit has fostered a normative characterization of a high proportion of domestic units, for instance, the view that lower class urban Negroes and single parent families are symptomatic of disorganization (Lancaster, 1961). The loaded term *incomplete family,* which is often used in the literature to refer to such domestic units, reflects this bias.

In the face of such confusion, it has been suggested that the concept of the nuclear family not be used, especially in kinship analysis. According to Lancaster (1961, p. 329), "it appears that there may be considerable advantage at this stage of research and analysis in looking at households and their temporary and permanent compositions: that is, in taking the point of view of the household as a building block of a system rather than the nuclear family." Levy and Fallers (1959) suggest the use of the concept *kin-structured domestic unit* as an alternative. This concept permits the size and composition of the residential unit to be an open empirical question.

The anthropologists' approach to the nuclear family is revealing by contrast. In the societies they study they usually find some pattern of institutionalized mating which provides a child with at least one social father and mother. In most societies people are able to distinguish from other kinsmen their social as well as their biological parents and siblings. Anthropologists would probably also agree that there exist small-scale domestic units often consisting of the mother and her child and sometimes the social (and/or biological) father. They would readily add, however, that this unit is often submerged into a larger one from which, from a structural point of view, it can be only analytically separated. What American sociologists are studying, then, are concrete, kin-structured domestic units which are culturally defined as the nuclear family. They seem to be proceeding from culturally determined, middle class values about the family instead of from the empirical composition of the domestic group.

What is commonly referred to as the nuclear family can most validly be studied by examining the kinship system in which it is embedded. Thus the domestic group can be considered as one structural unit whose members are recruited on the basis of kinship —where kinship refers to consanguineous and affinal relationships. The emergence of sociological interest in American kinship can be dated from the appearance of Parsons' (1943) seminal paper, in which he established a framework for the study of American kinship and examined the family in the broader perspective of kinship. As Adams (1968, p. 177) has correctly seen, Parsons was interested in the comparative and historical problem of the structural place of American kinship in society and its relationship to other systems. He was also concerned with describing the kinship system itself. It is this latter focus of Parsons to which we attend here.

Much of Parsons' argument rests on the terminological analysis of American kinship. He states, "It can perhaps be regarded as established that, with proper precautions, analysis of kinship terminology can serve as a highly useful approach to the functioning of social structure" (pp. 22–23). But terminological analysis, as the analysis of language as a system of symbols and meanings, is limiting specifically in that it reduces the examination of kinship to the examination of a cultural system. As Fox (1967, p. 243) suggests, kinship terminology indicates the way people classify their kinship universe and how they see their world of kin and is, moreover, an ideal classification of kin. Parsons' paper is thus an analysis of the cultural aspects of American kinship, and as such it is not directly concerned with patterns of behavior.

Our stance toward Parsons' approach as well as toward

that of his opponents (who will be discussed shortly)' is neither assent nor dissent. We take the position that the relationship of cultural to structural units is itself an empirical question—that both Parsons' approach and that of his opponents are valid ways to study kinship, yet they do not result in isomorphic pictures of kinship systems because they focus on different dimensions of a complex entity; error arises from the failure to recognize this. As Fox (1967, p. 243)' reports an analogous situation among the anthropologists, it seems we are in the presence of a common pitfall.

By examining the terminological system, Parsons came to the following conclusions, which became the basis of research. First, the American kinship system operates in terms of the principle of bilateral descent,[2] meaning that descent and hence kinship relations are reckoned through both lines of ego's nuclear family. Second, the system of descent is symmetrical. There is no structural (terminological)' bias in favor of solidarity with the ascendant and descendant families in any one line of descent, thus making an "onion" (sic)' structure the most distinctive feature of American kinship. Third, on the basis that there are no terminologically recognized kin units cutting across the nuclear family and that the nuclear family is the only terminologically recognized kin group, the American kinship system is made up exclusively of interlocking nuclear families, and the isolated nuclear family is the major structural unit of American kinship.

The ensuing debate about American kinship resulted from research findings at some variance with Parsons' analysis. Sussman (1959)', Sussman and Burchinal (1962)', Axelrod and Sharp (1956)', and others have challenged the isolation of the nuclear family thesis, pointing out that, structurally, this unit is embedded in a kin network of visiting and aid. Litwak (1959)' proposed the presence of a structure he terms the modified extended family, consisting of a series of domestic units joined together for aid and support. Farber (1966, pp. 69–78)' proposed that the ideal sym-

[2] Actually, Parsons discusses American kinship as bilateral in the first ascending and descending generations and as multilineal in succeeding generations in the sense that any number of lines of descent may be treated as significant. Bilateral descent is a correct description at the level of this discussion.

metrical pattern (onion structure) of American kinship is actually asymmetrical, locating the emphasis on the wife's line of descent.

Some distinctions must be made between Parsons' conclusions and the research findings of his critics. Parsons is concerned with American kinship in a comparative and historical sense. His analysis is based on kinship terminology, which indicates only very broadly the nature of a kinship system, and in a cultural sense moreover. Sussman, Litwak, and others have been studying the functioning of kin relations and have approached the problem from a structural, not a terminological-cultural, point of view in identifying regular patterns of behavior. In addition, in examining structural aspects of American kinship, these sociologists have made it into something it is not and have used concepts and approaches which could not describe the nature of these patterns of behavior among kin. Because these sociologists have not clarified the meaning of the nuclear family from a structural point of view, there is some question as to whether they have refuted Parsons' cultural concept of the isolated nuclear family by their research. They have not buried the concept by showing that kin relations exist outside the domestic unit. Parsons does not use isolation to refer to contact among kin, but rather to mean that the most stringent kinship obligations occur within the nuclear family and that contacts with kin outside this unit must be subordinated to its needs (Parsons, 1951, p. 186; Pitts, 1964, p. 89).

We have arrived at the point, then, where we have identified discrepant grounds of debate. We continue now with our critique by addressing some questions concerning the concepts used in the debate (and elsewhere in the study of family and kinship) and by discussing some broader issues which flow from these considerations.

The extended family, rigorously construed, is a structural concept used to study kin groupings where rules of residence favor a composite form of the family (Murdock, 1949, Ch. 1). As defined by Lancaster (1961, p. 328, employing the definition of *Notes and Queries on Anthropology*), an extended family is a kin unit, not necessarily living in the same household, in which two or more lineally related kin of the same sex, with their spouses and offspring, are subject to a single head with jural authority. As a tool for studying American family structure, Litwak (1959, pp. 177–78) defines the modified extended family structure as "a family relation consisting of a series of nuclear families joined together on an equalitarian basis for mutual aid." The concept as construed by Litwak is an attempt to indicate regularity in kin relations outside the domestic unit. As is quite apparent, it is in no way analogous to the rigorous anthropological meaning of the extended family.

The modified extended family concept probably should be dropped from the analysis of American kinship structure because for this purpose it is meaningless as Litwak defines it. Furthermore, any notion of the extended family is incompatible with the terminological (cultural) kinship system and with more generalized American value orientations. For example, in Cumming and Schneider's (1961) study, respondents not only defined the nuclear family as the ideal residential group but also believed that it should not be extended vertically or horizontally. In addition, according to Fox (1967, pp. 259ff for an extended discussion), our kinship terminological system seems to indicate great difficulty in actually forming extended families. Fox argues that the Eskimo terminological system (of which ours is a subtype) reflects a strong tendency in the kinship system as a structural entity not only to shrink socially significant kin but also to distort the generation principle necessary for forming extended families.

Let us now turn, in our attempt at conceptual clarification and critique, to Parsons' thesis that American kinship is ideally symmetrical and to Farber's thesis that it is actually asymmetrical. Parsons stresses the fact that no linguistic differences in kinship terminology would lead ego to treat his mother's line of descent differently from his father's. Farber (1966, pp. 69–78), on the other hand, states that the bilateral system tends to be structurally asymmetrical. What he probably means is that there is an emphasis on relationships with ego's mother's consanguines as indicated by evidence on socioemotional closeness to siblings and cousins. Parsons might well reply that residence patterns of kin groups tend to be neolocal. (Indeed, twenty years before Farber, Parsons (1943) did maintain that certain deviant behavior patterns may exist in American kinship but that these do not disturb the symmetry of the cultural system.) And the question should then devolve on empirical evidence. For Farber to argue the issue in terms of whether kinship

relations are symmetrical or asymmetrical is to apply a property of
kinship terminology, which is essentially where Parsons rests his
argument, inappropriately to the behavior of relatives in such a
way as to shift the grounds of controversy into an area where there
is confusion about what kind of evidence would settle the matter—
cultural-terminological or structural-behavioral.

Another much broader problem which can also be raised as
part of this critique involves a prevailing postulate which implicitly or
explicitly underlies most, if not all, sociological kinship studies—the
assumption that rights and obligations to kin are based on closeness
of consanguinity (Adams, 1968) or degree of relationship (Parsons,
1943)'. Research by anthropologists indicates that this assumption
is vague because closeness of kin or kinship distance has at least
three meanings to Americans. First, it refers to genealogical distance, meaning the number of intervening categories of relationships
and number of generations traced before a common relative is
found. Second, it means physical distance—the number of miles
or the hours it takes to travel from one house to another. Finally,
it means socioemotional closeness or distance, which can be anything
from a feeling of identity or difference to understanding or lack of
understanding to sharing or not sharing certain prestige symbols, as
Schneider (1968, pp. 72–73)' demonstrates. These considerations
direct the investigator to gather three kinds of apposite data to study
the influence of consanguinity on the quality of kinship relations—
and to account for them in some manner in the course of analysis.

Much of the above discussion indicates that the study of
kinship lacks analytically precise concepts. Now we must raise
another kind of question. Are we studying kinship at all or are we
studying family forms? This problem concerns the prevailing
tendency to use the nuclear family as the unit of kinship analysis—
to look at kinship relations by examining how families are related
to each other through horizontal (collateral) and vertical (intergenerational) extension, without distinguishing relationships among
individuals and without exploring other types of relationships. By
replacing nuclear family with kin-structured domestic units, as
Levy and Fallers (1959)' have done, we allow the actual composition of such units to be variable, and the entire matter of the basis

on which more complex familial forms are built becomes an open question subject to empirical verification.

A further problem, concerning the system referent when the domestic group is used as the unit of analysis, is the failure of investigators to distinguish between, on the one hand, approaches to domestic groupings in which the nuclear family is used as the basis upon which more complex familial forms are compounded (for example, extended families) and, on the other hand, approaches to the use of the nuclear family as a point of departure for analysis of kinship. In the latter, ego's relationship to immediate, nuclear kin is examined, followed by an examination of his more distant, nonnuclear kin (see Murdock, 1949, pp. 2–4, 92ff). The failure to make this distinction has been a failure to separate a kinship system from kinship groups. Although a kinship system may be used to recruit individuals to groups such as families, a kinship system is not a group, and it does not correspond to any aggregate of kin. It is a system of relationships determined by definitions of consanguinity and affinity. Thus, although a kinship system is not a compounding of families, it may be used as the criterion by which to compound such units (Murdock, 1949, pp. 90–93).

If it is admitted, with Parsons, that American kinship is composed of interlocking nuclear families (a conception of somewhat limited applicability to structural consideration of American kinship and at best a hypothesis), then in view of the above an attempt to delineate the structure of our kinship system from this starting point and with this unit of analysis could not in the nature of the case lead to its discovery.

To recapitulate, outside the broad cultural matrix in which American kinship is embedded and which indicates an ideal system (known terminologically) of bilateral or multilineal descent with the residential unit ideally defined as the nuclear family, sociologists have not delineated structural aspects of American kinship. And they have not explored factors which may account for the variability in the domestic unit. In addition to examining relations within the domestic group, sociologists have focused on how kinship is used to recruit more complex familial forms and kin networks of mutual aid and support in an attempt to disprove the thesis of the isolation of the nuclear family in American society. There is some question, however, whether such a focus is justified or whether some of the concepts employed are appropriate to refer to such aggregates. The thesis that the core of American kinship consists of interlocking nuclear families is a vague and, perhaps, a misleading guide for structural considerations.

Moreover, although sociological research indicates the prevalence of kin-structured domestic units and kin networks, the factors which may account for the variability we find in both have not been thoroughly studied. Some individuals have a wider range of kin than others. The nature of these relationships differs for different individuals. Often the wife's relationship with her kin is different from the husband's relationship with his. Some relatives are specifically excluded from some individual's network of kin. Others are chosen for frequent interaction. Such variations as these, and others as well, may occur by social class, age category, religious affiliation, and the like.

It is to the question of the variability in kinship relations that we address ourselves in the latter portion of the chapter. Consequently, before turning to the analysis of kinship relations as they occur among the members of our working class sample, it is necessary to set out something about the context of American kinship in the sense of the broad institutional matrix in which our kinship system is embedded, to consider the basis of choice in the recruitment of socially significant kin, and to examine such factors as social class and socioemotional distance insofar as they relate to kinship and to the recruitment of socially significant kin.

Regarding the institutional context of American kinship, Homans and Schneider (1955) point out that it is structurally differentiated from other social systems to a high degree. The only major kinship grouping is the residential unit ideally composed of the nuclear family. Aside from socialization, several of the more important functions of kinship are absent. For example, succession is absent in that a person does not attain office in any important sense simply through kinship. Inheritance is by testamentary disposition, which may or may not include kin, especially outside the domestic group. Furthermore, there is no binding descent principle that operates to form kinship groupings other than the domestic unit.

In comparison with the case in societies characterized as ascriptive, in American society the range of recognized kin is narrowly defined by individuals, and there is considerable variability among individuals in the number of recognized kin. Cumming and Schneider (1961) report that in their sample the number of recognized kin ranges from 34 to 280, with a median of 151, including the affines of the informant's consanguines but not the spouse's kin. The number of kin to whom the informants could gives names was about half the number they reported they recognized. One principle of American kinship which explains the comparative narrowness of this band of recognized kin has been noted: Of two ways of recruiting kin, Americans recruit by adding those related by marriage, such as spouses of consanguines, rather than by tracing back further to one's ascendents and then adding more distant collateral lines of these consanguines or by adding consanguines of one's own spouse (Schneider, 1968). These findings indicate some advantage in using the ego-centered approach to kinship, rather than in examining kin networks of families, which would submerge the individual variance apparently built into the structure of American kinship.

If indeed American kinship is structured along consanguinal networks to which spouses are added, this is a feature of fundamental and far-reaching importance—in a methodological sense, as we have indicated, and in a substantive sense as well. Rather than nuclear families, for instance, the kindred seems to emerge as one of the basic units of American kinship, a fact which has certain implications for the recruitment of kin for social interaction, with which we are concerned. The kindred structure allows an individual a great deal of choice in selecting kin with whom he will interact. For instance, according to Freeman (1961), such structures present the individual with a wide range of optative relationships—those which, in the absence of any binding descent principle, make it possible for him to assent to interaction as he pleases or as it serves his special interests. Or again, in societies like ours, where the modal form of interaction is in nonkinship contexts but where people

need or wish on occasion to rely on kin for aid and support, the
kindred, according to Fox (1967, p. 167), is useful. The independent importance of the kindred aside, it implies the existence of
particular kinds of criteria of recruitment, given the broader institutional setting of American kinship. Recruitment patterns must
comport with the norm of free choice, be flexible enough to ac-
commodate varied purposes for interaction, be receptive to occa-
sional as well as to sustained levels of interaction, and serve multiple
functions.

These criteria tell us something of the nature of the bases
for recruitment of socially significant kin. For example, the criteria
are congruent with the way our kinship system fits with American
equalitarian values. Choice (not incidence or prevalence, it should
be understood) of kin with whom to interact is not based on closeness of consanguinity alone. As Cumming and Schneider (1961)
found, this freedom of choice stands in sharp contrast with Firth's
(1956) results in his study of English kinship, in London, where
intimacy, or social significance of kin, was directly related to closeness of consanguinity. Thus, in the Cumming and Schneider study
of American kinship, some parents were excluded from those
informants considered intimate kin, and other informants gave
the same status to a sibling as to their own children. And in cases
of geographical propinquity, recruitment was based on compatibility.

If consanguinity alone does not govern intimacy among kin,
certain nonkin factors become important; and it becomes meaningful to question the effect of geographical dispersion of kin on
recruitment for interaction. Adams's study (1968, p. 22), repre-
sentative of many others, reveals that approximately 49 per cent
of the respondents' recognized kin lived within 100 miles of their
residences, while the remaining proportion was widely dispersed.
But the meaning of residential dispersion for recruitment is complex and appears to be related to social class. The dispersion of
kin actually indicates the residential mobility of the respondent as
well as his kin's mobility. This mobility in turn is related to the
respective occupational statuses of respondent and kin, white-collar
workers being modally more geographically mobile than their blue-
collar counterparts. In Adams's (1968, p. 24) sample, stable working class people and working class people who had moved up to

white-collar levels recognized more kin within a 100-mile radius than did working class people who had moved down from the middle class and stable middle class people. Class of origin, then, affects recognition of kin. The role residential dispersion plays in interaction with kin also depends on class-related variables. Adams (1968, p. 170) found that although the chances for wide residential dispersion of kin were greater for middle class respondents, it did not result in isolation from kin. On the other hand, residential separation and migration from kin by working class respondents, though less frequent, was likely to result in diminishing the kin network to the husband's and wife's respective parents. Adams (1968, p. 24)' also found class differences in why respondents moved. When working class respondents did move, it was primarily in response to unsatisfactory relations with kin, whereas white-collar respondents were geographically mobile in response to occupational opportunities and career demands. Adams's findings on working class kin networks are congruent with Young and Wilmott's (1957, pp. 114–16, 172)' conclusion that in London residence and kinship interact to solidify kinship ties in the working class, although Adams's findings on the middle class indicate that residence is not so important a factor in that class in recruiting kin for interaction.

Social class and kinship relations are also important to consider in connections other than residential dispersion and migration. For instance, much of the literature pertaining to the effect of class-related variables on kinship makes implicit assumptions which upon examination leave the whole matter of the effect of class an open question. One central issue is how far socially significant kin extend across class lines. According to Adams (1968, p. 161), the assumption that ego's socially recognized kin come from the same occupational level as ego's family of procreation underlies the debate over the presumed dissociative effects of vertical social mobility on kinship relations. By using the kin network of families approach, this literature does not effectively separate the husband's consanguines and their spouses from the wife's and implies that marriage occurs among class equals. Ample evidence (see Burchinal, 1964)' leads us to question this implication. Also inherent in this perspective is a failure to recognize that individuals may change their definition of which kin are socially significant over time.

For example, a person who has recently moved up in the occupational hierarchy may recruit more kin whose occupational status is similar to his new one. (At the very least, an ego-centered approach, and perhaps also the use of a concept like the kindred, would clarify many of these issues as well as permit a test of many such assumptions.)

The socioemotional aspects of kinship relations also assume importance because of the low salience of consanguinity as a basis of recruitment of kin in American society. A complex of socioemotional factors of closeness seem to influence the recruitment of socially significant kin. As has been pointed out by Schneider (1968), Cumming and Schneider (1961), and Parsons (1943), the expression of kinship in American society involves demonstration of diffuse solidarity, which may be expressed through a variety of activities and in a variety of forms. It involves friendliness, rites of passage, reunion, and the like. Ideally, it does not consist merely of aid but is a supportive, helpful, and cooperative relationship. It rests on trust and cannot be narrowly confined to a specific kind of behavior. To whom among one's recognized kin these feelings are directed and how they are expressed depend, in turn, on a variety of factors. Some of these have been discussed above. Others concern the structure of kinship relations itself, such as the tendency noted by Cumming and Schneider (1961) and Robins and Tomanec (1962) to recruit collateral kin rather than ascendents and descendents. As Cumming and Schneider (1961, p. 505) suggest, the less demanding and less obligatory collateral bonds are important in a society where the social structure is characterized by organic solidarity but where values emphasize equality and freedom of choice. Thus the "solidarity of the sibling group" (sic), characterized by sociability, is an important fact of the kinship system of the United States. But Cumming and Schneider base their findings on older respondents. The composition of ego's kindred, however, varies with age. It has been suggested that with ego's increasing age, the socially effective kin become in significant part his own generation. Such a shift in emphasis due to age may explain the "solidarity of the sibling group" for these older respondents. Additionally, sex may play a part, along with age, in patterning expressions of diffuse solidarity. The structuring of sex roles, especially that of wife in such a way that she becomes central in performing kinship-based duties, is important. And even here, moreover, we may find variability by social class in this female emphasis. (Again, it is important to recognize that these findings and hypotheses result from an ego-centered approach to the study of kinship.)

The most important fact in the recruitment of recognized kin for social interaction is that in our society ego has choices which are affected by age, sex, and class variables and are not based on closeness of consanguinity alone. A central characteristic of American kinship, as Schneider (1968, pp. 75-76) has maintained, is that a relative is first of all a person. Thus, the American kinship system should not be seen as a major structural consideration outside the domestic group. Variations in structural units of American kinship, such as are found in kin-structured domestic units and, perhaps, the kindred, are a consequence of class, age, sex, or similar variables, which are permitted by the vagueness of kinship symbols.

In concluding this overview of perspectives and issues in family and kinship studies, we may make the following observations. Sociological research on family and kin ties has not presented the evidence necessary to reject Parsons' thesis that the most stringent obligations to kin lie within the residential unit. Studies focusing on interaction among kin have demonstrated the ubiquitous presence of kin-structured domestic units—culturally defined as the nuclear family—and functioning kin networks. Anthropologists have found that in the United States wide variations in the number of recognized kin and in the selection of kin for interaction present difficult problems of analysis. Such variability is probably not due to a multiplicity of kinship systems but to a single-core system of kinship which permits much variation (Schneider, 1968, p. 114). However, sociological research has provided only a little empirical evidence to substantiate our belief in the above point of view. We know little, if anything, in a rigorous and systematic way about the variability that exists in the structure of kinship relations and the factors which account for this variability.

The fact that the American kinship system permits such wide latitude in selecting kin for interaction probably accounts for the looseness with which we conceptualize kinship variables and, perhaps, for the inappropriate use of others. In turn, we may fail to thoroughly recognize the effects of other variables and especially nonkinship variables on the structural aspects of American kinship. Sociological research has overemphasized the specific activities among kin to the relative neglect of the structure of these relationships. We have more knowledge of the types of aid and support given and received among kin than we have of which kin are socially significant and the way these relationships are structured by the broader institutional context of American society and by the larger kinship system itself.

Diversity in the structure of kin ties outside the domestic unit has not only led to the use of inappropriate concepts, such as that of the modified extended family, but has also prevented the examination of factors which affect the variability in the size and composition of kin networks. Most of the sociological studies of kinship employ the nuclear family group as the starting point. The concept of the kin-family network is vague precisely because it has as its referent modal kin relations of the domestic unit. A focus on the socially significant kinship universe of individuals, rather than on the domestic group, seems to be indicated. In an ego-centered approach, one would abstract a system of consanguineous and affinal relationships to the individual.

It is from this latter perspective that we approach the kinship relations of the members of our sample. Rather than taking the household as a point of departure and observing the social relations which members of a nuclear family or other domestically defined family form maintain with their relatives, we consider each respondent as an individual apart from the domestic arrangement in which he or she resides and conceive of his possessing a universe of consanguineous and affinal kin. For this analysis, we make a pragmatic decision about how much of an individual's kinship universe falls within our purview on the basis of whether the relatives of our respondents reside within the Philadelphia metropolitan area or beyond. By this procedure we do not forego treating a legitimate question: What is the relationship of domestic family forms to the social interaction of their members with the universe of their kin? Instead, we treat household composition as one factor among others whose impact on kinship relations, as the interaction between ego and his universe of kin beyond his household, is an empirical matter. The following analysis, then, delineates the sources of variability in rates of social interaction of individuals with members of their universe of available kin. We hope to shed some light on the question of working class isolation, or lack of it, from kin in middle and old age.

To the extent that measures of sheer contact may indicate isolation from kin or the lack of it, few members of the working class in this study are isolated if they have primary or secondary kin living outside their household but in metropolitan Philadelphia. Ninety per cent of the respondents have at least one such relative. Of these, only 18 per cent failed to visit or to receive a visit from at least one relative within the seven days preceding the interview.

The 1,596 working class respondents in our sample have among them a mean of approximately fifteen living primary and secondary kin outside of their households; 23,709 relatives all told. Of these primary and secondary kin, 14,806, or 62 per cent, reside in the metropolitan Philadelphia area and are the kin of 1,436 of our respondents. Of the remaining 160 respondents, 36 have no living primary or secondary kin whatsoever, and 124 have primary and secondary kin living beyond the metropolitan Philadelphia area only. In this chapter, we are concerned with those 1,436 working class people who have kin in the Philadelphia area and with the amount of interaction they sustain with them.

To measure the amount of interaction among kin, for our purposes three factors must be controlled: the geographic distance of relatives from respondents, the genealogical closeness or distance of relatives, and the number of relatives constituting the respondents' available kin network—that is, the number of primary and secondary kin living in metropolitan Philadelphia. In Table 14 relatives are arrayed according to whether they live on the respondent's own block, one to five blocks, or six or more blocks distant from the respondent's household (but within metropolitan Philadelphia). Within each of these geographical categories, relatives are divided into genealogically close and distant kin. Close kin are the respondents' parents, sibs, and children. All others are considered distant for our purposes. Relatives at each geographical and genealogical

remove are further characterized by the number of times they interacted with a respondent during the seven days preceding the
interview.

Table 14 clearly indicates that the rate of interaction with
primary and secondary kin is largely a function of proximity and
is only secondarily a function of genealogical closeness (as here
defined). For example, close relatives were seen less frequently,
on the average, if they live six or more blocks away from our
respondents than genealogically more distant relatives who live
one to five blocks away or on the same block. These results support,
for the working class, the contention discussed in the preceding
section of this chapter: The recruitment of socially significant
kin does not depend on closeness of consanguinity alone; propinquity is overwhelmingly more important.

We measure interaction with kin in a more refined manner
by a kin-contact ratio: actual contact over expected contact.
Actual contact is the number of contacts with kin the respondent
reports for the seven days preceding the interview. Expected contact is defined as follows:

$$\text{expected contact} = \sum_{i=1}^{6} N_i \overline{X}_i, \text{ where}$$

Where N_i = number of relatives respondent has in the ith cell of
geographical-genealogical kin distance classification,
Table 14

$\overline{X}_i$ = mean number of contacts in entire kin population
for all respondents taken together for the ith cell of
geographical-genealogical kin distance classification,
Table 14

Ratios larger than 1.00 are characteristic of respondents who had
more contact with their relatives than one would expect on the
basis of their kin network composition with respect to geographical
distance and genealogical distance; and ratios less than 1.00
are characteristic of respondents with less contact than one would
expect on this basis. Cutting points on kin-contact ratio scores

Table 14

Geographical-Genealogical Distance Classification of Primary and Secondary Kin in Metropolitan Philadelphia, by Frequency of Interaction with Respondents

(in raw numbers)

Geographical-Genealogical Distance	Number of Times Seen by Respondent During Past 7 Days									
	0	1	2	3	4	5	6	7 or More	$\bar{X}_i$	Total
Same block										
Close kin	9	31	4	4	4	11	11	93	5.0	167
Distant kin	67	115	43	31	4	21	7	199	3.8	489
1 to 5 blocks										
Close kin	95	160	88	39	28	24	6	97	2.6	537
Distant kin	444	448	232	99	32	51	10	198	2.0	1,514
6 or more blocks										
Close kin	1,286	1,175	192	108	32	36	15	106	1.0	2,950
Distant kin	5,495	2,799	399	211	56	67	21	101	0.6	9,149
Total										14,806

are distributed by approximately equal intervals around 1—
the expected value.[3]

DEPRIVATION

Pope (1964)' has reported that periods of deprivation and
Wilensky (1961) has maintained that disorderly career histories
restrict contact with kin. Moreover, the reduced amount of social
participation with kin which occurs at the onset of a period of
economic deprivation is held to persist far beyond the crisis situation
which initiated it. One assumption of this thesis is that changes
in the level of the wage earner's income throughout his career
are consequential for the rate of social participation with kin
living outside his household. We shall focus, then, on the financial
careers of working class people.

In attempting to estimate the nature of the income history
of the heads of households in our sample, we concentrated on the
years between 1935 and 1964. For each of six five-year periods
during this time interval, the respondent was asked, "How much
did you usually earn?" (The respondent was presented with a
card showing different weekly incomes, ordered in eighteen-dollar
increments and asked to tell the interviewer the letter which
corresponded to his average wage during the period in question.)'
His wages were converted into per capita family income, according
to the number of dependents he possessed in each five-year span
of time. The Consumer Price Index (CPI)' for Philadelphia
was then introduced into the computations by converting the
official index values in the 1965 *Statistical Abstracts of the United
States*, which were based on 1957 to 1959, to a 1935 to 1939 base.

[3] In all references in this chapter to the kin-contact ratio, the following ratio scores correspond to the designated category labels:

Much less than expected	0.09 or less
Less than expected	0.10 to 0.5
As expected	0.6 to 1.1
More than expected	1.2 to 1.9
Much more than expected	2.0 or more

Where the extreme categories have been collapsed the following labels are
employed:

Lower than expected	0.5 or less
As expected	0.6 to 1.1
Higher than expected	1.2 or more

For the six time periods, the least-squares regression coefficient of per capita income upon the converted CPI was computed for each respondent. (For convenience, the index as actually computed was a linear function of the regression coefficient, i.e., $\Sigma XY - (\Sigma X \Sigma Y)/N$, where X represents the time dimension and Y income.) A slope score representing per capita income in relation to the CPI curve was thus derived for the periods during which income was reported. It serves as an income history index revealing whether the breadwinner's per capita income increased more rapidly than did the rise in the CPI; increased, but not enough to keep pace with the increasing CPI; or decreased absolutely in per capita dollar value.

Before turning to an analysis of these individual indices, we can illustrate the over-all trends in income over time of several of the sizable cohorts of workers in our sample. Figure 1 illustrates the nature of these income histories (for 630 of the 698 bread-winners since the remaining sixty-eight cases, omitted for the sake of clarity, form a number of small groups and the resulting curves would have been unstable as groups). The solid, heavy curve in the figure represents the CPI for Philadelphia during the period covered, by reference to the index scale on the left abscissa. For purposes of visual comparison, the average per capita income for the 360 household heads who reported income during all six of the five-year periods in this study is illustrated as based upon income for 1935 to 1939; it is referable to the index scale or the dollar scale or both. Thus, the two curves are comparable; and a comparison roughly indicates the disparity, as a percentage of the 1935 to 1939 data, between the changes in per capita income and the cost of living as represented by the CPI. The curves for the other groups of respondents reporting income during fewer than the six con-tinuous five-year periods are also included in the graph. These are comparable with each other (and with the main group of 360 continuously employed) with respect to the average weekly income scale, although (for clarity of graphic presentation) they have not been scaled to a common index.

Figure 1 reveals the over-all inability of the portion of the working class sampled in this study to make large income gains over their working lives either with respect to the cost of living or in

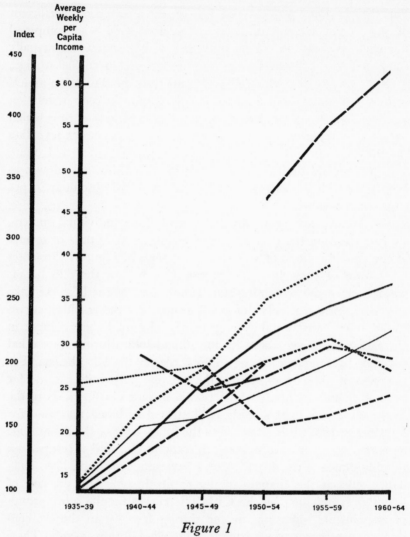

Figure 1
WORKING CLASS INCOME HISTORIES, 1935–64

terms of wages, considering the number of dependents the wage earner was supporting. (The uppermost curve in the graph, for instance, represents only five cases and is included here, even though it is an unstable curve by reason of the small sample, precisely because these five young breadwinners are apparently the only cohort in the sample with significantly high and rising average weekly per capita incomes over a reasonable portion of their working careers.) Only one other group has been able to maintain a rate of average weekly per capita income over the years which exceeds that of our group of 360 continuously employed (who, in turn, just barely fail to manage to keep pace with the increased cost of living). This group of workers consists of 123 people who retired between 1955 and 1959. The remainder of the breadwinners in the study, at one point or another, and for a relatively large span of their working careers, have income history curves which decrease relative to that of the 360 continuously employed breadwinners and, without doubt, relative also to the CPI, or else their wages start at such a low level of average weekly per capita income that the steady increase they show over time does not take them very high up the per capita income scale. For example, see the group of fifty-four breadwinners who ceased work between 1950 and 1954. One group in particular suffers a sharp decline in income between 1945 and 1954. It is composed of forty-nine individuals who, up to 1964, never regain their pre-1945 per capita level of income. Almost without exception, these men are veterans of military service who had larger than usual numbers of children after World War II, thus materially altering their chances to make per capita income gains during the years of their offsprings' dependency. (Their period of military service, for which no income is reported, is represented by the dotted line in Figure 1.)

In general, then, Figure 1 reveals that members of the segment of the white working class sampled in this study have been restricted throughout their adult lives to relatively low levels of per capita family income, whatever the absolute value of their income may have been. In these terms, then, it is unlikely that many people in our sample were at any time significantly more affluent than they are now, although, of course, they might have been justifiably termed solvent at a particular point in their lives. But here the virtually insoluble question of what was poverty or solvency in 1940, for example, raises its head. And this is by and large a fruitless question. Rather, the purpose of graphically illustrating the income history curves of the breadwinners in our sample has been to show that the current low level of income among our working class sample is rooted in their wage structures almost from the time they entered the labor force. Poor people in our sample as well as those with a modest but adequate income (whom we have termed solvent) may or may not have been born to parents with a low level of income, but ever since their early working careers they have remained in the ranks of those with relatively low incomes. Of course, by definition, our sampling procedure failed to net the upwardly mobile. But this sample has also not been sharply downwardly mobile from middle class levels of per capita family income—and we are sampling at the destination, so to speak.

Let us return now to the question of income history and contact with kin living beyond the household but within metro-politan Philadelphia. We consider the income history index scores of the poor and the solvent separately. Among those presently poor, we divide the breadwinners into three categories: those with slope scores indicating a per capita income gain greater than or equal to the increase in the CPI curve; those with any other slope scores which rise but at a rate which fails to match the rise in the CPI; and those with slope scores indicating declining income. Among the solvent, we divide the breadwinners into only two categories: those with positive slope scores greater than or equal to the CPI curve, and all others. We are interested in determining whether their solvency is being maintained relative to the cost of living. If not, any difference between those whose incomes are rising too slowly to keep pace with the cost of living and those whose incomes are simply falling is moot in view of their present solvency. In either case, they are downwardly mobile on an income dimen-sion but nevertheless still solvent. If the income of the solvent is rising compared with the rate of increase in the CPI, then this category of solvent people represents the possibility of significant upward mobility in a larger sense for those still in the labor force.

Individual income history index scores are available for 698 breadwinners (thirty-six additional breadwinners gave no answers to questions about income history). Table 15 arrays those of the 698 poor and solvent breadwinners who have primary or secondary kin in metropolitan Philadelphia by their kin-contact ratio scores. The Ns reveal that among poor breadwinners with relatives in metropolitan Philadelphia, the number whose income

Table 15

INCOME HISTORY INDEX BY KIN-CONTACT RATIO OF BREADWINNERS WITH PRIMARY AND SECONDARY KIN LIVING IN METROPOLITAN PHILADELPHIA
(in percentages)[a]

Kin-Contact Ratio	Income History Index				
	Poor			Solvent	
	Greater than or Equal to CPI Curve (N = 55)	Positive but Less than CPI Curve (N = 103)	Negative Declining Income (N = 36)	Greater than or Equal to CPI Curve (N = 117)	All Other Positive and Negative (N = 321)
Lower than expected	47.2	57.3	52.7	41.9	44.2
As expected	25.5	15.5	19.4	27.4	22.7
Higher than expected	27.3	27.1	27.8	30.8	33.0
Total	100.0	100.0	100.0	100.0	100.0

[a] Percentages may not add to 100 because of rounding.

has fallen over their lifetimes, relative to the CPI, is small. The majority of the presently poor have had rising per capita incomes over their working lives, but the rise has not kept pace with the increase in the CPI. However (and still looking at the Ns), about 28 per cent of those now poor have enjoyed income increases at or greater than the rise in cost of living during their working years. Also, among the solvent, we find an almost identical proportion of breadwinners, 27 per cent, whose incomes have kept pace with or have increased faster than the CPI. As we shall see later, although there is an age difference here, the poor being older than the solvent, age in itself is not related to scores on the income history index.

In view of the extremely powerful role of residential proximity in determining the rate of contact with relatives outside the respondent's own household, revealed in Table 14, we expect to find only moderate differences in the rate of contact with kin by other factors. But to the differences we do find, we are inclined to ascribe great weight. Thus, among the currently poor whose incomes have not risen enough over a large segment of their careers to keep pace with the CPI, we find the largest proportion of breadwinners who have less kin contact than would be expected (in view of their physical and genealogical distance from relatives and the number of kin in metropolitan Philadelphia who constitute their primary and secondary kin network). Among the poor with declining incomes over much of their lifetimes, we find the next highest proportion who see little of their kin. But the breadwinners whose kin contact is least restricted are now solvent. And their history of earnings since 1935 indicates that they have been able to maintain income at a rate equal to or exceeding the rising cost of living.

Thus, restricted contact with kin is indeed partly a function of a history of income deprivation. Additionally, current income standing also contributes to low contact with kin, once propinquity, genealogical distance, and size of kin network are taken into account. Of all those with income histories which failed to keep pace with the CPI, proportionately fewer of the solvent than of the poor have lower than expected kin contact. Lower than expected rates of kin contact are a function of present and past deprivation jointly. To have been deprived in the past and to be still deprived leads to the greatest amount of restriction of contact with kin. To have suffered no past deprivation and to be presently solvent yields the least amount of restriction of contact with kin. But to have been solvent in the past and yet to be presently deprived or else to have been deprived in the past but now to be relatively solvent (compared with the rest of the breadwinners considered here) leads to a degree of restricted contact with kin which is intermediate to that of the always deprived and the never deprived.

Although declining past and low present income levels lead to greater restriction of kin contact, the proportion of the deprived who have higher than expected rates of kin contact is not correspondingly reduced. Table 15 shows that the proportion of those who have more than expected kin contact remains about the same for every category of breadwinner, that is, regardless of present or past income level. This finding raises the question of the meaning of the restriction of kin contact which accompanies deprivation, a question to which we shall return shortly.

These findings, then, testify to a further aspect of variability in the recruitment of socially significant kin, an aspect which concerns the restriction rather than the expansion of the kinship universe for social interaction. Even when the powerful influence of propinquity is controlled and when account is taken of genealogical distance and the number of available kin, the degree of a breadwinner's past and present economic success influences his rate of social participation with kin. In other words, once certain obvious controls on kinship itself and on accessibility are imposed, the viability of kinship relations remains subject to social class factors. This is not to say, however, that class position per se influences the rate of kinship interaction. We do not have the data on middle class interaction rates among kin to permit cross-class comparisons. Had we such data, it might well turn out that once the same controls were instituted, lack of economic success would restrict kinship interaction among middle class people to a similar degree. This supposition would be congruent with the notion of a single-core system of American kinship. But the present data indicate that for the working class unsuccessful performance in the class system has as its correlative in the kinship system a measurable amount of shrinkage in relations. The recruitment of socially significant kin is in this sense subject to nonkinship factors linked to social stratification. These results strongly support the perspective on American kinship delineated earlier in this chapter. That is, a person's standing as a relative is only one component of his status set and, in terms of his social participation with kin, is not necessarily the most important component outside of his own domestic unit. Choices in interaction with kin include class-related factors which appear to operate independently of the powerful influence of propinquity. Of course, class-related variables do not figure alone in recruitment of socially significant kin; we consider other relevant factors later.

The thesis that deprivation restricts contact with kin has the corollary that the effects of unemployment are cumulative and persist even after episodes of job loss have passed (Pope, 1964). The explanation given is that the crisis of unemployment undermines self-confidence in social interaction and sets in motion a progressive weakening of ties to others wherein loss of self-respect promotes withdrawal, which further feeds feelings of low self-esteem, and so on in a vicious circle. On this assumption we would expect that more of those who have experienced unemployment in the relatively distant past would score low on the kin-contact ratio than would the recently unemployed. (Thus, we asked, "Were you ever out of work and looking for a job more than five months in a row? During which years?") This expectation is the case. Among breadwinners who ever have experienced a period of unemployment lasting more than five months, about a half of those 141 persons whose unemployment occurred before 1960 had lower than expected kin-contact ratio scores, while only about a third of the forty-six breadwinners whose unemployment occurred between 1960 and 1964 had low scores.

However, if a third category of breadwinners is introduced into the comparison, those who have never been unemployed for a five-month period, we find that 43 per cent of these people without any episodes of job loss score low on the kin-contact ratio. That is, their rate of kin contact is not substantially different from that maintained by the breadwinners who were unemployed before 1960. Apparently, then, those who should have been most restricted in their interaction with kin by virtue of the cumulative effects of unemployment are in fact little more restricted than those who never have been unemployed. And the least restriction of kin contact is evident among the most recently unemployed. This finding suggests that shortly after the crisis of unemployment the rate of contact with kin rises somewhat, perhaps as a function of assistance, sympathy and moral support, or attempts to find employment through kin. When the episode of job loss has passed, kinship relations subside but become essentially no more restricted than before. Rather than disruptions and discontinuities accounting for restricted kin contact in themselves, they seem to be quite secondary when compared with the long-term trend of income. And in the short run at least, unemployment reduces the amount of restricted contact with kin.

Possibly the contradiction between our findings and those of Pope and Wilensky arises because two different segments of the class hierarchy are considered in our respective studies. Pope refers to his factory workers as middle class, and Wilensky refers to his respondents as middle mass. They belong in a higher income bracket than our respondents. However, the contradictory findings may not be due to socioeconomic status differences between the two study populations but to the more rigidly controlled measure of kinship interaction we have employed here. At any rate, there is over-all agreement on the general proposition that past and present deprivation is associated with restriction of contact with kin. But disagreement exists on the more specific meaning of deprivation. Some would single out episodes of unemployment as the crucial variable, since they indicate career disruption and economic hardship, and would infer from this disrupted kinship relations. Our contention is that level and direction of change in income in relation to cost of living over a long period of time are the crucial variables; and income deprivation does not necessarily imply that kinship relations will be disrupted even though they may be restricted.

We now explore further the meaning of the restriction of kinship interaction which occurs under conditions of past and present economic deprivation. It will be recalled that a lower than expected kin-contact ratio score serves as the operational definition of restriction of kinship interaction. And it will be further recalled that while working class people presently poor and with a history of deprivation are more likely than others to have restricted contact with kin, their level of intensive (greater than expected) contact with kin is not thereby reduced. Neither, then, may kinship solidarity decline in the face of economic deprivation. This hypothesis assumes, of course, little or no relationship between kinship solidarity, considered as a form of socioemotional closeness, and rate of kin contact.

The question of kinship solidarity must be approached indirectly, in view of the well-known invalidities of respondent statements about feelings of closeness to particular relatives. Therefore, we formed a kinship solidarity index from items dealing with the existence of a charismatic relative; whether a residential move was ever undertaken in order to live near a relative; and sociability preferences, as between friends and kin.[4] On this index, we find that our assumption about the relationship between contact with kin and kinship solidarity is borne out. At every level of the kin-contact ratio, precisely the same proportion of working class people (both breadwinners and nonbreadwinners) score low, intermediate, and high on the kinship solidarity index. Breaking the extreme kin-contact ratio score categories each into two finer intervals does not alter the result: There is neither a prima facie nor a statistically significant association between kin contact and kin solidarity.

But the solidarity of our respondents with their kin is related to their income history. Poor and solvent respondents whose income has been keeping pace with or rising faster than the cost of living have the greatest proportion of people among them with a low degree of kinship solidarity (that is, with a score of zero on the kinship solidarity index)! Two-thirds of them as compared with about half of those with other income histories score low on kinship

---

   [4] The kinship solidarity index is composed of the following three items: "Is there *one* person, among all your relatives who is looked up to especially—in other words, someone that a lot of other relatives go to with their troubles and problems, and so on?" "Have you ever moved from one place to another so as to be nearer to any of your relatives?" "Which would you rather do when you want to be with other people: visit your relatives, visit your friends, visit friends and relatives equally, or stay at home with your family?" (Single choice only.) A respondent received a score of one for each of the following: a "yes" response to the first item above, a "yes" response to the second item, and any response to the third item except "visit friends."

solidarity. The largest proportion of breadwinners with the highest degree of kinship solidarity (that is, with a score of two or three on our index) is to be found among those poor people whose income has been declining in absolute dollar amount! Twenty-one per cent of them scored high as compared with between 6 and 7 per cent of those with other income histories. And the rest, poor or solvent, lie in an intermediate position between 21 and 67 per cent with respect to their scores on the kinship solidarity index.

The meaning of restricted contact with kin associated with an economically deprived career history is now a bit clearer. The breadwinners who have been so deprived perceive their universe of kin in a way that has led us to term them solidary; their upwardly mobile (in an income sense) working class peers are less often members of such solidary kin networks. Restriction of kin contact does not, then, imply withdrawal or retreat which stems from the loss of self-confidence in interpersonal family relationships. Rather, the connotation of these data is one of retrenchment and restriction in the sense of confining one's kinship relationships to the more supportive segments of one's kin universe. We infer that kinship relationships become a compensatory source of personal support when a man fails in his efforts to achieve in the economy.

Another aspect of kinship solidarity concerns the feeling that the family provides an adequate amount of companionship. Again, we asked the question indirectly by requesting the respondent to think of a person of his own age and sex who is better off than he. And then we inquired whether the respondent thought such a person had more family companionship than himself. (The question was: "Among all the men/women around here who are your own age, think of one who is better off than you are. Compared to you, does he have more family companionship?") This form of questioning establishes an economic reference by which to gauge feelings of family companionship so that respondents with different income histories may compare their satisfactions in relation to an ideal situation as they conceive it. By so diverting the meaning of the question, we hoped to remove the stigma of guilt and the feeling that one's family had been disloyal—feelings which may otherwise attach to negative answers to a direct inquiry about relatives and may lead to invalid responses. The respondent was thus able to

ascribe to his lack of economic success any perceived neglect on
his or his family's part. And, of course, this is precisely what we
wished to know. In addition, the item phrased in this way permits
a person to say so if he feels that he is better off than anyone he
can think of. In this manner, we can remove from consideration
those people for whom more or less family companionship is not
essentially connected with their general well-being as they define
it. The remaining respondents, who then are able to make a positive
or negative evaluation of the state of their family companionship,
one can assume, are indeed judging their kinship relations in a context which may be meaningfully analyzed along with their economic
standing.

    Although the responses to this question bear a statistically
significant relationship to the degree of contact with kin, measured
by the kin-contact ratio, the differences are small. Sixty-one per
cent of those with lower than expected contact with kin said somebody better off than they does not have more family companionship,
and 72 per cent of those with higher than expected scores gave
this response. This relatively small effect of greater kin contact in
increasing feelings of family companionship is consonant with the
relationship between the kinship solidarity index and the rate of
contact with kin just discussed. Here, as before, we infer that high
rates of kinship interaction do not necessarily mean that a person
feels appreciably more satisfaction with these aspects of his family
life. Additionally, the relationship between feelings of family companionship and income history, in general, tends to support what
we have just found in connection with kinship solidarity and a
history of deprivation. Those breadwinners with a deprived history
of earnings (the poor with negative slope scores and the solvent
whose slope scores either are negative or, if positive, fail to keep
pace with the cost of living) are most likely to say that somebody
who is better off does not have more family companionship than
they do. We interpret these differences as meaning that restriction
of contact with kin which occurs as an accompaniment of deprivation may imply a more solidary, supportive set of kinship relations
but certainly does not imply the disintegration of kinship ties as
has been heretofore believed.

Other factors, apart from past and present income deprivation, bear on the probability of a person's having a low kin-contact
ratio score—among them the composition and structure of the
domestic unit of which an individual respondent is a member. By
consideration of the composition and structure of the respondent's
domestic unit, we wish to open up for empirical scrutiny one of the
issues we raised in the first section of this chapter. If we permit
the actual composition of the domestic unit to be variable, rather
than considering variously composed units as nuclear families in a
single category, can we come to any conclusions about the basis on
which more complex familial forms are recruited among working
class people in middle and old age? Thus, in attempting to answer
this question, we look at the family forms which exist in the households of our respondents and consider the nuclear family as one
among several other domestic arrangements. And we also consider the marital status of our respondents. However, even with this
much elaboration our analysis is still limited in certain respects. Our
attention is confined to the universe of kin grossly conceived, rather
than to subsets of kin such as consanguines as opposed to affines.
Furthermore, because of the nature of our measure of kinship
interaction, the kin-contact ratio, we are not able to specify the
boundaries of the viable kinship universe of our respondents in
terms of ascendant, descendant, or collateral kin. Nevertheless, we
expect to be able to throw some light, in a general way, on the
question of recruitment of socially significant kin and the restriction
of kinship relations of working class people in nuclear families as
compared with those in other domestic units. In this special structural sense and only insofar as broadly defined social participation
is concerned, these data refer to the question of the isolation of the
nuclear family in American society.

Turning first to the relation between the marital status of
our respondents and their interaction with kin, we find that
significantly larger proportions of working class people who have
been separated or divorced from spouses or who have never married
have much less than expected (see footnote 3 above) contact with

kin than either those who are presently married or those who are widowed. While 16 and 17 per cent of the married and widowed, respectively, have much less than expected kin contact, 32 per cent of the thirty-one separated respondents, 39 per cent of the twenty-six divorced respondents, and 42 per cent of the seventy-four respondents who were never married maintain this low level of interaction with their kin. That is, over and above the relatively smaller size of the kin universe of people who are separated, divorced, or who never married, and taking account of their physical and genealogical distance from kin, the disruptions of separation and divorce and the lack of descendant and affinal relationships of those who never married restrict the rate of kin contact they sustain even more than widowhood does. Perhaps these are the consequences of negative sanctions attaching to disruption of the domestic unit or to never having formed a family of one's own in an unquestionably viable kinship system. The involuntary disruption, by death, of the domestic unit carries with it no such restrictions: The widowed and the married enjoy approximately similar rates of kin contact. But the severity of restriction of kin contact among the separated, the divorced, and those who never have married is indicative by contrast of the imposition of sanctions. To be separated still leaves open the possibility of reconciliation; the restriction of kin contact is not as great as it is for the divorced, for whom the probabilities of remarrying into the same kin line are remote. However, not to have been married is an implicit rejection of familism and, at our respondents' ages, most likely a permanent one. Accordingly, restriction of kin contact is most severe among people who never have married, and the proportion of them with much more than expected kin contact is the lowest of all.

For want of a better term, and with the understanding that despite its negatively loaded value connotation no such judgment is intended, these separated, divorced, and never married individuals have irregular marital statuses. Statistically, they are nonmodal in American society, and in a normative sense they are proscribed in American culture. Such departures from typical and ideal marital status restrict recruitment of socially significant kin beyond the domestic unit. These, along with other aspects of domestic family arrangements, constitute a set of factors separate from past and present deprivation which wreak effects on participation within a universe of kin. (However, they may be a function, in part, of such deprivation.) Of course, not every kind of irregular marital or domestic arrangement is necessarily accompanied by restriction of contact with kin. Those involved, our respondents and their kin, probably determine this by their own definitions of the situation. Thus, as we assumed above, in the culture of working class kinship widowhood is not defined as a marital condition to be sanctioned by avoidance, while divorce, separation, and never having been married may be normatively proscribed.

Let us turn to a slightly different index of irregularity in family arrangements, household composition. In Table 16, respondents are arrayed by the type of household to which they belong: whether they are the sole occupant of the household, whether they live with their spouse or with spouse plus children (nuclear family), and whether a spouse is missing from a household containing a parent and children. Respondents from these various households are ranked according to the proportion of them with restricted—that is, lower than expected—interaction with kin as measured by the kin-contact ratio. There is in Table 16 a substantial variation in the proportion of respondents with restricted participation in their universe of kin. About 32 per cent of the solitary females have restricted participation with kin, while about 60 per cent of the solitary males are so restricted. Between these two extremes lie those respondents who come from households where the culturally ideal form of domestic unit exists, conjugal pairs or nuclear families. (Among those 952 respondents classified as domiciled with nuclear families are seventy-three individuals who are members of nuclear family units with whom other relatives reside.) Those family household arrangements associated with greater restriction of kin contact for their members are either nuclear families lacking a female spouse or nonindependent conjugal pairs (families in which one of the conjugal partners is living with other relatives—thirty-nine cases—and conjugal partners who both are domiciled with other relatives—forty cases). And solitary males have the highest rate of kin-contact restriction. The character of these most restricted of families conforms to what has frequently been observed of older working class men. More often than women,

Table 16

HOUSEHOLD COMPOSITION BY LOWER THAN EXPECTED
KIN-CONTACT RATIO SCORES FOR ALL WORKING CLASS PEOPLE
WITH PRIMARY AND SECONDARY KIN
IN METROPOLITAN PHILADELPHIA

Household Composition	Number	Per Cent
Solitary males	57	59.7
Nonindependent conjugal families	79	53.2
Nuclear families minus a female spouse	21	47.6
Conjugal pairs and nuclear families	952	40.8
Nuclear families minus a male spouse	131	31.3
Solitary females	161	31.7
Other	35	57.2

they are isolated from their kin, most notably, as Komarovsky (1962, p. 337 *et passim*) shows, from their married children.

Families less restricted in their contact with kin are all female headed. They consist either of females living alone or of a mother and her children without her husband. Their relative immunity from severe lack of kin contact may stem from the assistance rendered by her kin to a mother struggling to raise children or provide a home for as yet unmarried children in the absence of her husband. And perhaps the kinship bond among working class males is in general not nearly so strong as among females. The much publicized extreme isolation of the solitary working class female does not appear to be borne out insofar as kinship relations are concerned. The solitary lower class male is in a relatively much more serious position with regard to restriction of contact with his kin.

What is striking about the range of kin-contact restriction, insofar as it can be considered a measure of relative social isolation from kin, is the fact that the culturally ideal form of domestic arrangement (people residing as members of nuclear families or conjugal pairs) yields neither the least nor the most restriction of kinship interaction. This finding offers no compelling support for researchers who maintain that nuclear families and conjugal pairs are integrated into viable networks of social relationships with more distant kin. Members of female-headed nuclear families and solitary females experience less restriction of social relations with kin than do those whose domestic units are, with respect to cultural injunction, more complete. That form of domiciliary arrangement which guarantees the least isolation from kin apparently cannot be identified unambiguously by proponents of the idea that nuclear types are embedded in an active kinship system. Students of the family who hold to this position have also failed to specify which types of domestic families would exhibit more isolation from kin than the putatively integrated nuclear arrangements. An accounting of the kind needed would obviously have to make use of class-linked factors such as deprivation and income history, discussed above, and sex, as Table 16 illustrates, and their mutual relationship. Emphasis on domiciliary form alone is not enough. One very pragmatic consideration which no doubt has prevented such an elaboration is that many researchers investigate the social structure of family networks without controlling the joint and confounding influence of propinquity, size of available kinship universe, and genealogical closeness of kin. Without such controls, isolation measures based essentially on frequency counts are bound to be misleading as clues to the structurally patterned relationship between domestic family type and a wider circle of relatives.

On the other hand, these data also render no firm support to those who maintain that the nuclear family is isolated in the sense that obligatory relationships are strongest here and less so beyond the household. If there is a connection between the stringency of obligations within the nuclear family domestic unit and interaction with relatives beyond the nuclear family, it does not presuppose a particularly high level of isolation of members of such units from a wider universe of kin. Table 16 shows that four of the seven categories of households exhibit higher rates of restricted contact of their members with kin than that for nuclear families and conjugal pairs. It is difficult to discern what rationale that flows directly from the Parsonian position offers a convincing interpretation of these findings. Had nuclear family members or members of conjugal pairs exhibited the highest or the lowest rates of restricted contact with kin beyond the household, perhaps it would have been possible to adduce a reasonable accounting. But the apparent indeterminacy of the position of members of these households compared with residents of other kinds of domestic units makes most available interpretations tenuous at best. The culturally ideal form of family domiciliary unit is simply one among an array of different types in the working class, and the members of these households relate to their kin in ways which depend on nonkinship factors and perhaps also on hitherto undiscovered units of the kinship system.

Thus, in spite of the limitations of these data on family household units, they indicate that probably the most profitable course is to hold with the approach we discussed earlier in this chapter, one which leaves aside large elements of most current interpretations of American family and kinship. If there are in fact units of American kinship which integrate individuals into the kinship system beyond the household, they probably are not units of the kind so far described by investigators in this area. In addition, a major problem these data raise is how to account for the variation in kinship interaction observed in the working class in the face of the culture of the American kinship system. As was mentioned early in this chapter, a wide range in the choice of kin for interaction exists; this range is reflected in the data presented so far. And we have discussed some dimensions along which variability occurs. But the limitations of our sampling and instruments prevent us from proceeding further than these first steps.

Another form of family irregularity stems not from disrupted marriages and certain kinds of household arrangements but rather from the nature of the breadwinner's job. He may work irregular hours or have done so in the recent past. In consequence, his availability for interaction with kin outside his own household is confined to times of the day or days of the week when his relatives are unavailable. A total of 463 breadwinners were in the labor force during 1960 to 1964, and they were scored on an index of irregular working hours.[5] First, an exceptionally high proportion

[5] For each of the five-year periods of employment covered in this

of the 1960 to 1964 labor force, 42 per cent, scored high or medium on this index. And second, as we would expect, those with high or medium scores on this index are more restricted in their contact with kin than are those with low scores. Thus, of the fifty-five breadwinners with high scores on this index, 51 per cent had lower than expected contact with kin as measured by the kin-contact ratio. Of those 138 breadwinners with medium scores on this index, 55 per cent had lower than expected contact with kin. But of the 270 breadwinners with low scores on the index of irregular working hours, only 40 per cent had lower than expected kin-contact ratio scores. Incidentally, the distribution of kin-contact ratio scores for this group of breadwinners with low irregularity of working hours is identical to that of the rest of the sample, which was not in the labor force in 1960 to 1964.

RELIGION

Finally, the only other major variable which has even a moderate relationship to contact with kin, as measured by the

study, going back to 1935, we asked three questions, from the responses to which an index of irregular working hours was formed. If the respondent held a full-time job during a given five-year period, he was asked, "During this time, did you ever have more than one job at the same time?" (yes or no). He was then asked, "When you were working in that five-year period, would you say you worked Saturdays or Sundays all the time, most of the time, seldom, or never?" And finally, he was asked, "How about shift work in that five-year period. Did you always work shifts, most of the time, seldom, or never work shifts?" The following patterns of responses received the weights indicated. If a man had more than one job during a given time period and worked weekends and shifts his score was zero. A man received a score of one if he held more than one job and worked weekends all or most of the time but seldom or never worked shifts; or if he worked shifts all or most of the time but seldom or never worked weekends; or if he did not hold more than one job but worked weekends all or most of the time and also worked shifts all or most of the time. A man received a score of two if he held more than one job and seldom or never worked weekends and seldom or never worked shifts; or if he held only one job and worked weekends all or most of the time but seldom or never worked shifts; or if he held only one job and seldom or never worked weekends but always or most of the time worked shifts. And a score of three was given if he held only one job, seldom or never worked weekends, and seldom or never worked shifts. For present purposes, zero and one scores will be termed high irregularity of working hours; a score of two will be termed medium irregularity; and a score of three low irregularity.

kin-contact ratio, is religion. Those with the highest proportions among them with restricted kinship relations—that is, with lower than expected kin-contact ratio scores—are Protestants and Jews (48 per cent each as compared to 36 per cent for Catholics), while Catholics are least restricted, proportionately, in their contact with kin (37 per cent of them have higher than expected scores compared with 31 per cent of Protestants and 24 per cent of Jews). These data do not bear out the often noted familism of Jews, at least not to the extent that sheer contact with kin may be an indicator of it. Those professing other religions, including atheists, agnostics, and people who replied that they had no religion, are essentially no different from the Catholics in their kin-contact ratio scores.

NEGATIVE FINDINGS

In the preceding sections of this chapter, we found a small number of characteristics of working class people and working class social subsystems which bear moderate relationships to the restriction of contact among kin. If we leave aside the more general meaning of the specific constellation of factors associated with restricted kin contact, the strength of the relationships disclosed indicates the nature of working class kinship systems.

The system of working class kinship seems extraordinarily viable. Doubtless this viability is partly due to the easy accessibility of kin living in the city and partly to the numerosity of relatives, which produces a high level of kin per capita. These factors result in a set of relationships with relatives which in many respects is subject to extrafamilial influence. Additionally, the overwhelming effect of proximity on frequency of contact with kin suggests (as does the importance of the structure of the neighborhood for friendships, which was discussed in Chapters Two and Three)' that a good deal of the arena of working class social life is restricted to the close neighborhood. In addition to these situational factors and the disruptions of irregular working hours, only a small group of structural considerations—economic success, composition of the domestic unit, and religion—play any part in the recruitment of socially significant kin. Beyond this, individual choice plays some role, the strength of which cannot be ascertained here. In addition, though it is difficult to estimate, what might be termed *overload* may be significant. Given the facts that the majority of kin live at some distance, six or more blocks, from our respondents and that approximately 47 per cent of the universe of kin of all our respondents are not seen at all during the week preceding interviews (see Table 14 above), there is room for speculation that sheer numerosity of kin may make intensive contact impractical. But once this limitation has been recognized, it is still necessary to state that we have in working class kinship relations a systemic phenomenon. Not everything which could conceivably relate to restriction of contact with kin or expanded levels of kin contact in fact bear a relationship.

Hence, it is not surprising to find a large number of fundamental conditions and characteristics which might be expected to have significant effects on kinship contacts from a common sense point of view having no influence whatsoever on our respondents' kin-contact ratio scores. For example, poverty and solvency in themselves have no effect on kin contact. Nor does age, even though we consider the very old (those between seventy-five and seventy-nine) separately from people between sixty-five and seventy-four. And when age is controlled, poverty and solvency remain unrelated to working class kin contact. This finding reinforces our earlier contention that restriction of kin contact is a function of a history of income deprivation for breadwinners and not of present economic standing alone. But it also brings into question the whole notion of role losses which accompany aging and their relation to kin contact.

We saw above that the role loss accompanying widowhood did not restrict kin contact, widowed and married people both having identical distributions on the kin-contact ratio. Aging in itself, as a general indicator of status and role loss, has just been seen to be unrelated to kin contact as here defined. And if we look more closely at other indicators of role loss, we find similar relationships. Thus, for example, dividing up breadwinners and past breadwinners into their various standings in relation to labor force participation, we find no difference in kin contact whether a man is fully retired and not looking for a job, is retired but still looking for some employment, is retired but holding a part-time job, is working full time, is working part time even though he is not of retirement age, or is unemployed.

These findings, in combination with the evidence discussed in Chapters Two and Three concerning friendship relations, constitute a powerful argument for the irrelevance of theories of withdrawal or disengagement from social relations in the later years of life. Not only does aging per se fail to reduce kin contact, but also the role losses which accompany aging do not in themselves bear on either the frequency of kinship or friendship relations in the segment of the urban working class sampled in this study. On the basis of our data, we are compelled to suspect that previous findings on the relative isolation of the aged are artifacts of physical proximity, size of kin network, and distribution of close and distant kin among available (geographically proximate) relatives. It is quite possible, of course, that a broad class difference exists in patterns of association in later years and that withdrawal is a function of aging in the middle but not in the working class. Although it would be foolish to deny this possibility out of hand, at the same time the evidence which would force one to entertain it seriously does not seem to have been gathered.

Several additional hypotheses concerning restriction of contact with kin were tested. For example, downward intergenerational mobility does not restrict kin contact even though a history of income deprivation is related to lower than expected kin-contact ratio scores. The career mobility of our respondents is likewise unrelated to kin contact. On the subjective side, neither the number of perceived interclass moves nor the direction of perceived interclass mobility makes a difference in rate of kin contact. In our further search for socioeconomically related conditions which may bear on kin contact, we examined recipients and nonrecipients of various forms of welfare assistance. Again there was no discernible differences in kin contact.

Other major social attributes also fail to correlate with kin contact. Differences by education are negligible. Only about 8 per cent more of those with four years of high school or some college than of those with eight grades or fewer of schooling have restricted contact with kin. Immigrant status also is unrelated to kin contact;

no differences in kin-contact ratio scores were found among immi-grants or among first, second, or third generation citizens. And when we examine specific countries of birth, exceedingly small differences, on the order of 6 per cent, among national origin groups are found. And these appear to be functions of religion as much as of national origin.

Several attitudinal variables were examined for their possible relation to kin contact. We asked respondents to rate their ability to provide for themselves and their families and to rate the condition of their health; we formed a perceived disease index by asking whether the respondent thought he had any of a list of common diseases; and we asked several questions about how lonely the respondent feels, at present and in relation to the past. None bore any relation to kin contact.

Several practical considerations were taken into account. Car ownership, for example, scarcely reduces restricted kin contact or increases the proportion of people with greater than expected contact. Whether during the past week a person left his house more, less, or the same amount as he usually does also fails to affect his kin-contact ratio score.

And finally, we sought to ascertain whether a general syn-drome of interpersonal social activity may be related to rate of kin contact. By multiplying the number of friends with whom a person was in contact during the preceding week by the number of reported contacts with friends we arrived at a frequency measure. People with no contact with friends were also included. This measure bears no relationship to kin-contact ratio scores. Furthermore, as a check on this indicator, we asked about a series of common social activities, and after finding whether the respondent engaged in them during the past week, we questioned him about who was with him when he did these things. Again, these scores bore no relation to kin-contact ratio scores. Evidently, kinship and friendship networks are separate and divorced social subsystems in the working class. We can find no evidence that compensatory kinship activity is engaged in by those isolated from friends or that those who see little of their kin make up for a presumed lack of social relations within the extended family by seeing more of their friends.

The problem of working class isolation from kin is not a problem of isolation in a strict sense. Rather, the issue concerns the restriction of interaction with relatives in the universe of kin. For not only do 90 per cent of the working class people in our sample have primary or secondary kin living in metropolitan Philadelphia, but almost all of them did receive or pay a visit to at least one of those relatives, living outside their own households, during the week preceding the interview. Moreover, even within metropolitan Philadelphia, the geographical distance from the residences of kin is a powerful determinant of the rate of interaction between kin— more so than genealogical degree of closeness.

In view of the powerful effect of geographic proximity and the secondary effect of genealogical closeness on the frequency of kin contact, a ratio measure was devised to account for these factors and, in addition, for the size of an individual's kin network. On this basis, restriction of contact with kin in the working class was found to be a function of a history of income deprivation combined with present poverty. Poor people whose per capita family incomes, although rising, had not kept pace with the cost of living since 1935 and poor people whose incomes had been declining absolutely in dollars had lower than expected rates of contact with kin. Others presently solvent or presently poor but with incomes rising sufficiently to keep pace with or to exceed the cost of living have less restricted contact with kin.

Additionally, a history of unemployment before 1960 leads to more restricted kin contact than does having been unemployed since 1960. Yet those who never have been unemployed are in contact with kin at about the same rate as those unemployed before 1960. Thus, recency of unemployment results in an initially higher level of kin contact, most likely of a supportive nature to the unemployed person, following which extended family interaction subsides. The episodes of job loss experienced by working class people are not as potent a factor in restricting kin contact as the long-term trend of family income.

The observation that those most restricted in their contact

with kin do not have a correspondingly lower than usual rate of intensive kin contact led us to explore the meaning of restricted interaction with kin in terms of solidarity with relatives living outside the respondents' households. We found that family solidarity bears little or no relation to rate of interaction with kin. But solidarity and income history are related. Low kinship solidarity is a characteristic of the more successful families. And high solidarity is most often found among the poor people who have been most deprived all their working lives. Extended family companionship may well become a compensatory source of personal support for those who have failed economically. Other attitude indicators of close family feeling support these conclusions.

Another cluster of conditions, related to irregular family arrangements and disruption, also restricts contact with kin. The separated, divorced, and never married have lower rates of kin contact than do the married or widowed. Males domiciled alone, men raising a family without their spouses, conjugal pairs living with other relatives (or one of the conjugal partners living without his or her mate but with other relatives) all contact their kin less than do more conventionally domiciled families and also less than do female-headed families and solitary females. Moreover, disrupted family life, as distinct from irregular domestic arrangements, is associated with restricted kin contact. Those who work irregular hours or at unusual times of the week see less of their kin than do breadwinners with conventional hours of work.

And finally, Protestants and Jews are more restricted than Catholics in their contact with kin.

Age and poverty in themselves, taken separately or jointly, are not related to kin contact in this working class sample. Likewise, the role losses accompanying age—indicated by widowhood and retirement, for example—are unrelated to contact with kin. These findings constitute arguments against not only a role-loss theory of isolation of the aging but also against withdrawal theories, of which the disengagement variety is one example. Further, neither intergenerational occupational mobility nor career mobility are correlated with kin contact. Nor are several attitude configurations, including feelings of loneliness, related to interaction with relatives. And last, we could find no evidence that rate of interaction with friends is associated positively or negatively with kin contact.

These empirical findings have been elaborated in the setting of a general perspective on American kinship relations. That is, we have raised questions about the adequacy of present formulations concerning the isolation of nuclear family members from kin and the viability of kinship networks beyond the domestic unit in American society. By synthesizing information and theories about the cultural system of American kinship with some data on the patterns of kinship interaction, we took the position that kinship organization itself is only one of several factors affecting the recruitment of socially significant kin. Equally important, if not more so, are nonkin variables related to class, age, sex, religion, and irregular domiciliary arrangements. The unit, if any, of American kinship which influences social participation with kin beyond the households of our respondents remains to be discovered. The problem of the relationship between the system of American kinship and the patterns of recruitment of kin, which were illustrated in this chapter, remains a major task for research. The range of factors affecting the system of recruitment bears out anthropological theorizing concerning the wide degree of choice afforded relatives in defining socially significant kin—a degree of choice, moreover, which is hardly influenced by closeness of consanguinity. That this pattern of interaction comports with general cultural orientations concerning individualism, egalitarianism, and pluralism is probably true. But left unanswered are important questions concerning the kinds of variables, such as age, which do not fall within the range of factors affecting recruitment. More precise information about social and cultural system linkages in kinship is needed.

Attitudes Toward Social Class

Miranda. *'Tis a villain, sir,*
I do not love to look on.
   Prospero. *But as 'tis,*
We cannot miss him. He does make our fire,
Fetch in our wood, and serves in offices
That profit us. What, ho! slave! Caliban!
Thou earth, thou! Speak!

SHAKESPEARE
The Tempest

155

At various points in the preceding chapters we have alluded to the possibility that our respondents may hold certain attitudes. We did this as an aid in interpreting some of the results of our analysis of friendship patterns and association with kin. We mentioned, for instance, that poverty may facilitate the development of an orientation toward neighbors which enables the poor to cope more successfully than solvent people with the problems of establishing neighborhood friendships in localities where many people are economically dissimilar to themselves. In another instance, when interpreting the patterns of age homophily among poor and solvent, we speculated that the pessimism of the poor about their economic chances may have led them to maintain the kinds of friendships which would lessen invidious comparisons and the risk of personal rebuffs from those with better life chances. And again, when discussing the relationships among kinship solidarity, contact with kin, and a person's economic history, we implied that those who have failed economically may feel compensatory satisfaction in intimate family relationships. Thus, in these and other places in the preceding analysis, we have reckoned that certain of the patterns of social relationships found among the members of our working class sample may be understood in connection with their attitudes toward the economy and toward class phenomena. In this chapter we focus directly on these attitudes. They may furnish a further rationale for the patterns of friendship we have described earlier and thereby enable us to understand the relationship between economic standing and neighborhood contextual dissonance. But in addition an explicit study of the attitude configurations of members of our working class sample may throw light on the conceptions of class and class-linked phenomena of people who have reached the end of the competitive road. Those who are no longer directly involved in the occupational world may have quite different views about the hierarchical aspects of society depending on the relative degree of success they have attained. One implication which arises from studies of the class consciousness of American workers concerns the degree to which the ethos of achievement mitigates class feelings—one can always hope, in other words, that success will come in the future if it has not yet been attained, especially in a society which places such heavy emphasis on continual striving as the road to reward. But when the possibility of future effort in the economy has been eliminated by age and retirement, what does the working man think about a system in which he has had a modicum of success or in which he has not done as well as his age peers? We turn in the following pages to these and related questions.

One fundamental aspect of class perceptions colors many beliefs and attitudes about socioeconomic hierarchies in our society: the extent to which the society is believed to be open or closed to individual striving and to the achievement of occupational and monetary reward. Militant conceptions of class interest, support of political parties or candidates dedicated to class-linked programs, espousal of doctrines calling for redistribution of wealth, beliefs that the social system is founded on injustice, and willingness to overthrow the political system or to advocate such action—all these doctrinaire attitudes depend in some degree on whether a society is conceived of as open or closed by its members. And such a belief in turn no doubt depends on the economic experiences of the people in question and on the presence of differential rewards and other social contrasts in their environment. We shall examine these two putative preconditions of belief in the openness of society.

We sought two indirect ways of assessing whether our working class respondents believe the society is open or closed. In the first, we wanted to anchor their attitudes in their experience. Accordingly we asked them about their careers: "Over the years since you left school, do you think it became any easier for you to get ahead, harder, or did it stay about the same?" And immediately following their responses, we probed for the reasons: "Why do you say that?" The answers were recorded verbatim. We later classified the many different reasons into six categories: open system responses, semi-open system responses, closed system responses, aleatory responses, responses indicating an inability to form an image of the class system, and a residual category of other responses. If an individual gave multiple responses, each one was classified separately.

Open system responses were composed, predictably, of

statements to the effect that an opportunity was presented to earn more money or to take a better job or to continue or complete schooling which was or was not taken advantage of by the respondent. Some of these answers were quite general. An individual would state that he had a good chance to raise his wages and took it or simply that he took advantage of opportunities which were present. Others were quite specific in their statements, saying, for example, that they worked hard and trained themselves for a particular job requiring a certain skill. The general implication in most of these statements was that the opportunity for betterment was in the environment; only a few people spoke about their careers as if they had created some opportunity for advancement by their own hard work. We infer from such responses, then, that these people have an open society in mind when they think of their own working lives. In such a society the opportunities are provided, and one may or may not grasp them.

A small minority of responses fell into the semiopen category. Perhaps the chief interest in these responses is that they represent such a small percentage of the total, as we shall see below. Here we placed answers which indicated that the system is basically open but that if there are obstacles to the improvement of a person's economic standing, they may be overcome by remedial action on the part of unions and the government. Unions are mentioned as having helped to improve job and working conditions and enabling people to advance monetarily. Benefits accruing from military service were mentioned, especially since they enabled some of our respondents, through veterans' home loan programs, to buy a house they could not have afforded otherwise. Some looked upon social security benefits as a means of personal advancement.

Closed system responses were aggregated from quite varied response categories, but they had in common the underlying meaning that the system or the society is inadequate and hence individual failing cannot account for lack of success. Some people referred to machinery and automation as destructive of jobs. One man, pointing to his own career, said, "They need less skilled workers when they put in machines." Another voiced the cry of the intellectual Luddite when he said in connection with automation, "They should stop new ideas." Other closed system responses made explicit reference to some economic conditions or to the economy in general which indicated that a person's lack of success is a function of the business cycle. People who felt this way would point out, for instance, that their wages do not go up with the price of food. Others mentioned rising taxes in the face of rising costs of living. But the fiscal aspects of the economy were not the only ones which seemed disadvantageous. Other closed system responses stressed the availability of job opportunities in general as a function of the economic system. This question is not one of automation's replacing workers by machines but rather a recognition that an imbalance exists between people and places in the system as a whole. One man said there were not enough jobs to go around so that opportunities were scarce for him. Another put it this way: "Too many people—not enough jobs." All such comments were made in a context which clearly indicated that the respondent, while referring to his past experience, had a system referent in mind. Additionally, the indictment of the system as being responsible for their failures extended to other institutions—in particular to education. These respondents were, of course, referring in some sense to their lack of education and training, but they saw their situation explicitly as a function of the larger society and placed blame on the organization of educational opportunities in general rather than at their own doorstep. One man said, "There are more children than ever before and they are being better educated, so the average man is out." And finally, as one might expect in a study population of older people, some of the respondents referred to what they consider injustices arising from the inconsistencies of age grading in the economy. As one man put it, "people live and work longer" and contribute to job scarcity. Another said, "Retired people take jobs the younger should have." Some blame employers for unrealistic expectations about older workers and imply a lack of flexibility in the economy to adapt jobs to age-related changes in the individual: "At age forty-five you are too old for some jobs; at fifty your mind is too rusty to learn something new."

An additional category of responses to the open-ended probe can best be termed aleatory. Some working class people said that success or failure was due to luck. But more did not use that word. Instead they gave reasons which plainly indicated the operation of

chance factors in their lives. Some of them cited their own health
or sickness in the family. The responses of these people indicate that
their advancement was largely out of their own hands. Yet they did
not feel that getting ahead was a question of opportunities or lack
of them as a function of the larger society. For them there was
plainly an element of randomness about their progress or lack of it.

The aleatory responses differed, however, from another type
of answer to our probe. Even randomness or the chance factors just
mentioned presume that our respondents have the notion of a
framework within which social mobility is possible. However, the
responses of some people seem to deny that they hold this image of
the class order and movement within it. That is, some of our
working class respondents seem unable to formulate an image of
a society in which people do or do not get ahead. They did not
give irrelevant answers, for they understood the question well
enough to feel that their responses bore upon it. Their remarks simply
indicated no personal experience meaningful to the notion of getting
ahead. And indeed, a number of these respondents did say that
over the years their advancement seemed to stay about the same.
One man said, "Well, I always worked hard." Another said that
he "had the same job all the time." Such conceptions should not
be lumped into a miscellaneous residual category.

In the second approach we took in our endeavor to elucidate
attitudes toward the openness of the class system, we attempted to
divorce the response from explicit connection with an individual's
own success. We wanted our respondents to look at working class
people in general and to look at them, moreover, in the perspective
of the future. Relatively successful people may have good and
sufficient reason for believing that the society is open with respect
to their own careers. But if they see the evidence of failure around
them, their judgment about the prospects for working people in
general may be quite different. And similarly, for those who have
not gotten ahead, a judgment based on individual failure may
not extend to working people as a whole. So we asked a question
parallel to the preceding: "In the next ten years, do you think it is
going to be easier for working people to get ahead, is it going to be
harder, or stay about the same?" And again, we probed: "Why do
you say that?"

We classified the responses to this probe in the same categories as those developed for the item concerning the individual's own career. Open system responses indicate a belief that in the future opportunities will be available to the working man and that his ability to get ahead will depend upon whether he avails himself of the chances provided. One man said, "If he has the ambition and education, he can work and move ahead." Another man was more explicit, "Things improve every day, schooling gets better, they will be able to get better jobs with higher pay."

Other responses fell easily into the semiopen category. Some people believed that in the future special governmental assistance will help working people surmount whatever barriers may exist. Thus, "if the government helps people it will be easier." Or, "the government will provide jobs in the future." Others were more specific. One man said, "It has to do with the antipoverty program." And another said, "They are starting to train the very poor."

Again, the closed system responses were varied but fell mainly into the same subcategories in which we classified the preceding answers. Modernization and automation continuing to destroy jobs was one theme. One man said, "Machinery will take over more and more." And another echoed, "Machines will take the place of men." Other respondents cited what we have termed the business cycle. For instance, one man said, "I don't see how they can get along—it costs a lot of money to live when you have so many bills." Also, education seemed important to many. "More education is required than a working man can get or get for his children" was one pessimistic response. Another said, "It will be difficult unless you have specialized training—everything is education." And he went on to imply that he did not think the chances for more education would increase in the future. In addition, a few responses referred to the continuation in the future of the injustices of age grading and speculated that the sheer scarcity of jobs would persist. But we found one new subcategory of closed system responses. A few people foresaw restriction of opportunity for the working man of the future because of the competition from Negroes entering the labor force. One man said, "Too many Negroes in school; after they get out there won't be enough jobs for white people." Another simply stated, "Negroes are getting ahead of us."

We again encountered aleatory responses. Although nobody said that luck would determine the ability of working people to get ahead in the future, several respondents implied that no rational device and no individual effort could promote advancement in the future for working men. One said, "Nothing will do any good." Another said, "No remedies will help." Still others responded by indicating that in the future getting ahead would depend on highly individualistic or idiosyncratic factors. For instance, one man said, "It depends on the person."

And, as before, some respondents seemed unable to formulate an image of working people and their ability to get ahead in the future.

As one might expect, when we asked working class men who had found it easy to get ahead over the years why they thought their progress had been smooth, the great majority of their replies fell into the open system category. And those men for whom getting ahead was harder as time went on also responded predictably in the great majority of cases by giving closed system answers when we asked why their advancement had been difficult. Thus, the subjective dimension tapped by anchoring beliefs about the openness of the society in the individual's judgment of his own success appears to be fairly consistent at this level of respondent awareness. That is, even though the definition of what constitutes getting ahead has been left to each respondent and even though there is doubtless a wide variation in such definitions, we are content to assume this individual variability as a given since it produces a fairly consistent picture of the relationship between personal awareness of success or failure and the open or closed nature of the larger system in which it has occurred. Subjective upward mobility appears to our respondents to be due to individual effort in seizing opportunities the society presents and subjective downward mobility to the closing off of opportunities—a situation which also appears to our working class men to be inherent in the society.

Neither those who see the society as open nor those who see it as closed feel that by individual effort alone do men get ahead or fail to succeed. The closest one comes in these responses to strictly individualistic images are among those working class men we have classified as holding an aleatory conception of mobility. But even these answers contain no hint that individual effort would succeed for any other reason than chance. The sense of the openness of the society among these working class men, then, does not conform to the putatively middle class ethic of individual striving and achievement—an ethic which has the connotation that individual effort does matter, that to some extent at least a man makes his own opportunities. Rather, the picture which emerges in the segment of the working class sampled here is one of passivity. The implication is either that by and large getting ahead is out of one's hands since the opportunity to do so is denied by the very workings of the larger society or else that a man's efforts, if he believes himself to have been successful, require favorable social conditions to begin with. If a man does not emphasize such favorable conditions as a function of the society, he most often reverts to explanations of his achievement centering on luck or chance. Thus, working class men, of the age and income bracket we are dealing with here, do not deny or decry individual striving as efficacious but they think of effective individual effort as depending upon the larger structure of economic opportunity in the society. If a man feels that he has gotten ahead, then he says the opportunities were there; if he feels he has had difficulty in getting ahead, then he says the system did not offer any opportunity because of the way it was structured.

INCOME HISTORY

The relationship between a man's image of his success or failure and the image he holds of the openness of society, as we have said, is to be expected. But having affirmed this consistency of attitude, we may turn to an examination of the conditions which lead some to think of the society as open and others to see it as closed. And since our working class respondents were asked to look back over a long period of their own lives when thinking of getting ahead, we may compare these attitudes with the breadwinner's family income over a thirty-year period since 1935. To what extent do our respondents have perceptions of the class system which parallel their own monetary history? To find out, we will employ the income history index discussed in the preceding chapter.

Let us look at the income history patterns of the bread-

winners to seek some relationship between their feeling of having
gotten ahead and their actual accomplishment in terms of income.
In response to the question, "Over the years since you left school,
do you think it became any easier for you to get ahead, harder, or
did it stay about the same?", our breadwinners display no overwhelmingly strong association between the actual direction of earnings and feelings of ease in getting ahead. For example, about a
quarter of those breadwinners who are now poor and whose income
has been declining for much of their working lives feel it has been
easy to get ahead. And of those poor breadwinners whose income
has been rising, but not fast enough to keep pace with the increasing cost of living, exactly one-quarter feel it has been easy to get
ahead. As might be expected, we also find that those presently poor
or solvent whose incomes have been rising faster than the cost of
living have the largest proportion (slightly over one-third) of breadwinners among them who say that it has been easy to get ahead.
So there is some correspondence between subjective and objective
indicators of upward mobility. We cannot say with any assurance
why this correspondence is not greater. However, these people, in
the great majority of cases, were in the labor force in the 1930s,
during the depression. More than likely, therefore, when they are
asked to reflect on the course of their careers, one of their salient
recollections is the difficulty of those times. Thus in comparison with
the hardships of the 1930s, even the poverty in which some of our
breadwinners have lived since then may be perceived of as being
easier.

The modal category of response for all breadwinners, except
those in grinding poverty (those whose per capita family income
has declined over the years)', indicates a feeling of stability. About
40 per cent of these breadwinners, with the exception just noted,
say that conditions have stayed about the same with respect to
getting ahead. And this is not as surprising an attitude for this
working class sample as it may seem at first glance. We have mentioned at various points in the preceding chapters a number of
elements of stability in the lives of our respondents. For instance,
we know that many of them are relatively long-term residents in
their present neighborhoods. Furthermore, our sampling has restricted, by definition, eligible respondents to those who now are and

have been blue-collar workers for most of their lives, so that people who have been occupationally mobile across the manual-nonmanual line do not fall within our purview. In addition, the income ceiling tends to eliminate from our sample those who have made great monetary gains while remaining in blue-collar occupations. Thus, several significant areas of our breadwinners' lives have not changed appreciably. And it is these areas that our respondents may have in mind when they say that the degree to which they have gotten ahead has remained about the same over their lives.

The most striking aspect of the relationship between income history and perceptions of getting ahead can be seen among the poor who say that their advancement has been hard since they left school. Almost half, 45 per cent, of those poor breadwinners whose incomes have declined over the years, about a third of the poor breadwinners whose incomes have risen but have not kept pace with the cost of living, and almost as large a proportion, about 29 per cent, of solvent breadwinners whose incomes have either been declining or have not risen enough to exceed the increasing cost of living maintain that it has been hard to get ahead. But still, those in grinding poverty, those with declining earnings, have the most substantial proportion of breadwinners who are aware of hardship. This latter income history seems to represent a tipping point, so to say, at which income decrements impinge on the awareness of large proportions of people. Poverty alone or poverty such that over time a man's income falls increasingly behind the cost of living apparently is not enough to make a very substantial proportion of these bread-winners aware that it is becoming harder to get ahead.

As we would expect, these poor breadwinners whose incomes have been declining also voice the largest proportion (62 per cent)' of closed system responses. This high percentage is approached only by that (40 per cent)' of the solvent breadwinners whose incomes have failed to keep pace with the rise in cost of living or else have declined. For the rest, only about a quarter of the responses are of the closed system type. Belief that society blocks the strivings of individuals is strongest, by and large, among those with a history of declining income whether they be poor or solvent presently— though, of course, such a belief is more prevalent among the poor. Correlatively, the largest proportions of responses indicating an image of a society open to individual advancement can be found among those whose incomes have been rising at a rate exceeding the cost of living—almost half of the solvent breadwinners' responses and 45 per cent of the poor breadwinners responses in this income history category.

The small proportion of responses which fall into the semi-open category represent a particularly interesting phenomenon. Less than 4 per cent of the breadwinners in this working class sample believe that over their lifetimes the government or unions or other agencies of the larger society have assisted in overcoming obstacles to individual advancement. Yet almost all these breadwinners have lived as adults through the period of social legislation and simultaneously of the rise of unions to great power which began in the early 1930s with the advent of the New Deal. Apparently, those who think it has been easier to get ahead do not make the connection between the opportunities available to them in the economy and the intervention of government and labor in the economic process itself. Whatever awareness may exist of the attempts of government to provide opportunity to the working man, it does not appear in the responses to this item. Possibly the linkages between broad social policy and the programs which implement it and the experiences in the labor market of any particular individual are so tenuous and indirect that it is unrealistic to expect people to perceive them when they reflect about their own careers. And, as we mentioned above, those blue-collar workers whose situations have improved radically over their working lives and who may on the basis of this experience be expected to perceive most clearly the impact of government or unions are not represented in our sample. Thus, working people such as those under study here may have no compelling reason to suspect that they have been assisted in some way by government or labor organizations. But aside from this possible lack of awareness these breadwinners may have made a tacit judgment of the effectiveness of government and organized labor in terms of programs and policies which bear on their own careers and ability to get ahead. Our respondents may have decided that from the perspective of their own lives such programs have been a failure.

Aleatory responses from our working class breadwinners

appear with greater frequency than do the semiopen responses just discussed, although not so frequently that we would want to characterize our respondents' conceptions of the class system as aleatory to any great extent. Aleatory images are most prevalent among poor breadwinners whose incomes have been rising but not fast enough to keep pace with the increasing cost of living. About a quarter of them believe chance factors account for their own economic advancement. Precisely this combination of rising income and decreasing purchasing power may well give rise to a feeling that one's own efforts count for little. One justification for apparent success, in the form of increasing income, which does not purchase an incrementally higher level of living and raise these working class people out of poverty, is that the system works at random and that getting ahead in more than a merely nominal sense is due to chance rather than to effort. By contrast, those poor breadwinners whose income is increasing more rapidly than the cost of living have the smallest proportion (5 per cent) holding aleatory images of the class system. They and their upwardly mobile counterparts among solvent breadwinners are most likely to see the class system as open. Their incomes are rising, and this increase yields tangible rewards in increased purchasing power. People whose own efforts yield maximum rewards may reasonably disavow chance or luck as the basis for their advancement.

And finally, the data reveal that in the main somewhere between 10 and 15 per cent of our breadwinners seem to be unable to formulate an image of the class system. The exception to this pattern is the group of breadwinners in grinding poverty, of whom only about 5 per cent are in this category. In a perhaps too simple sense of the term *class consciousness*, those who most lack income reward are the most conscious of the class system. Insofar as these data indicate, the poor breadwinners in the most desperate straits with respect to income are not apathetic, ignorant, or unable to formulate a conception of a socioeconomic hierarchy. On the contrary, these underdogs place the blame for lack of advancement squarely on the class system and, where their own careers are concerned, have the least difficulty of any group of breadwinners in conceiving of the operation of the society in terms of class factors. Whether those who are in grinding poverty also identify themselves more strongly than others with a particular class (a more conventional meaning of the term *class consciousness*) is a separate question.

But the perspective of these breadwinners' own life histories is only one dimension of the kind of awareness of the class system manifest in this working class sample. We also asked about the ability of working people to get ahead in the next ten years. The responses to this item are remarkable for the amount of pessimism displayed. No matter what the path of our breadwinners' income histories has been, between about 64 and 79 per cent of the responses indicate that these breadwinners hold conceptions of a closed class system for the immediate future of working class people. As in the preceding responses, those in grinding poverty give the largest proportion of closed system responses, and those solvent breadwinners whose income is declining absolutely or rising but not fast enough to keep pace with the cost of living give the next largest proportion of closed system responses. But the overriding import of these data is the relatively small amount of faith of the segment of the working class sampled here in the equalitarian nature of our society in the near future. Only about a quarter to a third of these responses envision an open class system in the future for the working class. And somewhere between about 5 and 15 per cent of the responses indicate that these breadwinners hold a semiopen image of society for the future.

A detailed analysis of the closed system responses to this item reveals that the modal response is a belief that automation will close off job opportunities in the future for working people. And the next largest subcategory is the belief that in the future educational opportunities and training for working class people will be inadequate. These two responses together account for well over half of the closed system answers in every income history group. The business cycle per se, the lack of jobs alone, and the competition from minority groups do not figure significantly. Plainly, what our working class breadwinners fear will close off future opportunities most is that combination of factors which, more than anything else, reflects the transition to a highly technological economy: technological replacement of heretofore useful skills and lack of access to education and training in a quantity and with a quality sufficient to guarantee some measure of job security.

The meaning of these closed system responses deserves further analysis. What we have seen so far is the impact of relatively successful or unsuccessful histories of earnings on working people's perceptions of the class system. Whether our respondents are asked about their own careers or about the future chances of working people in general, the less successful a person's history of earnings (as measured by our index) the more likely is he to see the class system as closed. And when asked to think about the future opportunities of working people, the great majority of all breadwinners, regardless of their income histories, see a closed class system, although a differential is preserved between the more and the less successful breadwinners in the absolute proportion of closed system responses.

However, since the breadwinners in this working class sample include those who are still in the labor force as well as those who are now retired, it behooves us to ask whether the perception of a closed class system is the reflection of the current lack of success of active participants in the economy or the resentment of retired people who no longer have the opportunity to make monetary gains in the labor force. If it is the younger employed working class people who express the view that the class system has been closed to them so far and will be closed to working people in the future, then we must interpret the foregoing data as a negative judgment on the structure of opportunity in American society by those trying to make their way within it. We would have, in this case, one indicator of working class discontent with the avenues provided by the economy for the attainment of success. If, on the other hand, closed system responses come predominantly from the retired, those over sixty-five, then perhaps it would be more appropriate to infer an attitude of resentment on the part of these older people. Their perception of the open or closed nature of the class system is hypothetical in the sense that they are no longer in a position to be rewarded or punished for economic performance. Of course, this

does not mean that the images of the class system held by our older
retired breadwiners are trivial in terms of this analysis. Depending
on the course of their history of earnings, our aged breadwinners'
images of the class system provide invaluable information on the
end result of successful or unsuccessful economic participation in
terms of its implications for democratic ideology. But the point we
wish to stress here is that the meaning of the closed system responses
of the retired does not carry with it so strong an implication of
discontent with things as they are. At least in principle, only those
still in the labor force believe that they are efficacious in the class
system.

In Table 17 we compare the closed system responses of
breadwinners over sixty-five and of those sixty-four or less. These
are arrayed by income history index score. Our interest in Table
17 lies not so much in the absolute magnitude of the percentages
but in whether the proportion of closed system responses of one age
category exceeds that of the other and whether the difference
depends to any extent on income history. The cell Ns in parentheses
below each percentage figure in the body of the table denote the
number of respondents in that age category with the particular
type of income history indicated in the upper stub.

The most general conclusion which can be drawn from
Table 17 is that when we ask our breadwinners to think of their
own experience in getting ahead, no matter what their actual
advancement in terms of income has been, a larger proportion of
the younger than of the older people's responses are indicative of a
closed class system (with one exception). Thus, the discontent of
those still in the labor force rather than the resentment of the
retired is reflected in these closed system responses.

The exception to this finding concerns breadwinners who are
currently poor but whose incomes have been rising at a rate equal
to or exceeding the cost of living. Only a very small proportion
(about 14 per cent) of the responses of the younger among them
indicate a closed system image, while about one-third of the responses of those over sixty-five indicate a closed class system. Those
who are still working and, although presently poor, are manifestly
getting ahead would of course have the least reason to perceive
obstacles to advancement. But their retired counterparts can do

Table 17

BREADWINNERS WHO PERCEIVE A CLOSED CLASS SYSTEM WHEN ASKED ABOUT THEIR OWN ADVANCEMENT BY INCOME HISTORY INDEX AND AGE
(in percentages)

| | Income History Index | | | | |
| | Poor | | Solvent | | |
Age	Greater than or Equal to CPI Curve	Positive but Less than CPI Curve	Negative Declining Income	Greater than or Equal to CPI Curve	All Other Positive and Negative
65 or more	32.0 (50)	27.5 (91)	47.0 (17)	19.7 (61)	32.4 (111)
64 or less	14.3 (14)	32.0 (25)	72.0 (25)	33.3 (66)	43.3 (238)

little more to increase income in a major way and thus are more likely than the younger breadwinners to see a closed class system even though they too, while currently poor, have had a history of rising income.

Although the results are not quite so clear cut as those in the preceding question, the responses of breadwinners currently in the labor force tend in the main to be more pessimistic than those of the retired about the future chances of working people to get ahead, as shown in Table 18. Among solvent breadwinners, no matter what their income history, a greater proportion of the answers of the younger than of the older are indicative of a belief that a closed class system will prevent working class advancement in the future. And likewise, among the presently poor breadwinners, those still in the labor force whose incomes have been rising, but not fast enough to keep pace with the cost of living, also are more pessimistic about the future of working people than their retired counterparts. But among poor people with declining incomes we find over twice as many closed system responses on the part of the older retired persons than the younger ones. And there is virtually no difference between retired and employed breadwinners who are poor now but whose incomes have been rising at a pace equal to or greater than the cost of living.

Table 18, then, shows that declining income over a long span of time is required for the retired more than the employed to see future opportunities closed off for the working class. Older, retired people in grinding poverty give the largest proportion of closed system responses of any group, and their younger employed counterparts the smallest. But also, those aged breadwinners who are poor but whose incomes have risen at a rate greater than or equal to the cost of living do not see future working class opportunities closed off any less frequently than do younger breadwinners with the same income history.

From the preceding analysis we should not conclude that age alone accounts for the relative conservatism of the retired. The fact that the image of a closed society is found, in the main, proportionately more frequently among the younger than among the older breadwinners would support such a view only if the evidence were derived from a longitudinal rather than from a cross-sectional

Table 18

Breadwinners Who Perceive a Closed Class System When Asked About Working People's Advancement in the Next Ten Years by Income History Index and Age

(in percentages)

	Poor			Solvent	
	Income History Index				
Age	Greater than or Equal to CPI Curve	Positive but Less than CPI Curve	Negative Declining Income	Greater than or Equal to CPI Curve	All Other Positive and Negative
65 or more	66.0	61.5	117.6	59.0	58.5
	(50)	(91)	(17)	(61)	(111)
64 or less	64.3	72.0	52.0	78.8	81.1
	(14)	(25)	(25)	(66)	(238)

study. What the above data do suggest, however, is that regardless of whether there is any inherently age-specific trend for people to think of society as closed, there is a correlative temporal association which links the image of a closed society not with aging per se but rather with the old person's history of earnings. And further, this association between income history and the image of a closed society depends on whether these breadwinners are thinking of obstacles to their own past economic advancement or to working people's advancement in the future. For continued, and doubtless also self-evident, failure to make income gains impels the aged more than the younger breadwinners to see society as closed in the future to working people's advancement. But such failure to increase income does not incline the aged more than the young to perceive society as having been closed with respect to their own past careers. On the contrary, the retired in grinding poverty give fewer closed society responses than do those still employed.

We must take cognizance of two general arguments before ascribing the patterns of response we have discussed earlier in this chapter to the economic history of our breadwinners. The first of these is the argument from differential perception of poverty. That is, it is conceivable that those in grinding poverty, who so much more than the others see that their own economic advancement has been hindered by a closed class system and who also most foresee a closed society in prospect for working class people, are more aware of the personal costs of poverty than are their poor counterparts with different income histories. And by the same token, it is conceivable that the closed system responses of the solvent breadwinners, which closely approximate those of the other poor breadwinners not in grinding poverty, also derive from a similar level of awareness of the personal disadvantages of relatively low income. In other words, all breadwinners, except those in grinding poverty, may have a similar level of awareness that their economic resources are inadequate for their needs. And this awareness may lead them to perceive a closed society. To check this possibility we asked our respondents to rate their current ability to provide for themselves and their families on a ten-point scale ranging from "very poor" to "very good." If some differential perception of the meaning of their economic position and its history is influencing the responses we observed earlier, then we should expect that those in grinding poverty will in some way be distinguishable from the rest of the breadwinners. The data demonstrate that those in grinding poverty are not any more aware of the personal costs of their economic position than are the other currently poor breadwinners and, in fact, are a bit less aware than their poor counterparts with rising incomes which nevertheless fail to keep pace with the rising cost of living. All the currently poor, then, have about the same proportion of breadwinners among them who are aware that their ability to provide for themselves and their families is "poor" or "very poor"—between 40 and 50 per cent. But among the solvent breadwinners, no matter what their income history, only from about 10 to 17 per cent think that their ability to provide is "poor" or "very poor." Thus, the awareness of the personal costs of poverty is not a function of income history but of current income standing.

The second general argument which may be raised about the pattern of responses described earlier is the argument from differential social origins. That is, the class of origin of those in grinding poverty may differ from the class of origin of the other breadwinners. For instance, they may be downwardly mobile people whose parents were middle class. And the combination of having fallen from middle class origins and having suffered harsh deprivation throughout their careers may cause them to view the society as inherently closed to economic advancement. Or, they may stem disproportionately from farm families, and their perception of the class system as closed may be a reflection not only of a history of income deprivation but also of the often noted shocks of adjustment to which working class families of rural origins are subject in urban areas. The data would seem to lend little support to this contention because there is a general similarity of class of origin of most of the breadwinners. The overwhelming majority of these blue-collar breadwinners are themselves children of parents who held blue-collar jobs for most of their lives. For poor breadwinners with incomes rising faster than the cost of living, about three-fourths stem from working class families. For all other breadwinners, about two-thirds have working class origins. Farm origins can be attributed to only between about 9 to almost 15 per cent of the breadwinners with different income histories, which amounts to virtually no differential

among them. The differences in the proportion of the downwardly
mobile with varying income histories are modest at best. All, except
those with incomes which have risen faster than the cost of living,
have among them between about 16 and 19 per cent with white-
collar fathers. The poor whose incomes are rising faster than the
cost of living stem from the middle class 11 per cent of the time,
while the solvent with the same income history stem from the middle
class about 23 per cent of the time. This is not a very striking
difference. However, it is equally important that those in grinding
poverty are not at the extremes of any of these percentage distributions. They are, with respect to fathers' occupations, no different from most of the breadwinners with other income histories.
Apparently, then, class of origin bears little if any relationship to
income history.

Given the relationships just discussed between income history
patterns and awareness of the personal costs of poverty on the one
hand and social class of origin on the other, we would not expect these
latter two factors to distinguish among those who see the society
as a closed system to any further degree than income history does.
The economic experience of the breadwinners in this sample, as
represented by their income histories, remains an important source
of variation in their images of the society as being open or closed.

NEIGHBORHOOD ECONOMIC CONTEXT

At the outset of this chapter we stated that two factors
may influence people's beliefs about the open or closed nature of
the society. The first, their economic experience, has just been discussed. The second, the nature and salience of differential rewards
within their effective environment, will be examined now. In order
to do so, we return to the neighborhood structural context as
descriptive of our respondents' effective social environment. We
focus on all the male respondents in our sample, including those
breadwinners excluded from the analysis of the preceding sections
of this chapter because no income history information was available
for them. Although the case base for some categories of respondents
is small because we examine many factors simultaneously, we proceed keeping in mind that our interpretations of the findings are
more suggestive than conclusive.

Table 19 arrays the proportions of working class men sixty-five or more who perceive a closed class system when asked about their own advancement over their working lives. The responses are displayed according to the poverty or solvency of the respondents, the wealth of their neighborhoods, and their friendship patterns. The numbers in parentheses below each percentage indicate the respondents who fall into each income, neighborhood, and friendship category. The perception that the class system is closed appears to be uniformly a function of the wealth of the neighborhoods. Poor and solvent old men, isolates as well as those with friends in the neighborhood, and even those whose friends live beyond the local area, give greater proportions of closed system responses if they live in poor neighborhoods than if they live in the wealthier areas. A poor old man in an impoverished neighborhood sees no evidence around him that others have become relatively more affluent than himself, and thus he can easily believe in the closed nature of the class system as it applies to him. But a poor man living in a neighborhood where others are wealthier is confronted with evidence that a degree of economic success greater than his own can be and has been attained by others. He then has less reason to believe that his own lack of affluence is due to barriers inherent to the society. Moreover, the poor man in a relatively well-to-do neighborhood has a residual increment of noneconomic reward. He may think that while he is not as well off as his neighbors, he nevertheless lives in the same area as more successful people. In some indirect sense and apart from the evidence provided by the relative affluence of his neighbors that it is possible to attain greater economic reward, he may convert his presence among wealthier people into some small sign of his own success, even though he lacks comparable income. On this count also, he may be less inclined to think of the class system as closed.

A situation somewhat analogous to that of the poor exists for the solvent old men. But the meaning of the comparison between the respondent and his neighbors is not quite the same. His image of the class system probably stems from the realization that his neighbors have not advanced to his financial state. In such a situation, he may not give so great a weight to his own relatively successful position as being a function of an open class society. He probably

Table 19

POOR AND SOLVENT MALES, AGE SIXTY-FIVE OR MORE, WHO PERCEIVE A CLOSED CLASS SYSTEM WHEN ASKED ABOUT THEIR OWN ADVANCEMENT BY MEAN NEIGHBORHOOD INCOME AND FRIENDSHIP PATTERNS

(in percentages)

Friendship Patterns	Poor			Solvent		
	\$4,000 or Less	\$4,001 to \$5,000	\$5,001 or More	\$4,000 or Less	\$4,001 to \$5,000	\$5,001 or More
	Mean Yearly Family Income of Neighborhood					
Isolates	36.4 (11)	38.9 (18)	26.0 (23)	33.3 (12)	31.5 (35)	13.0 (23)
Friends beyond the neighborhood	25.0 (4)	10.0 (10)	16.6 (12)	75.0 (4)	25.0 (20)	7.7 (13)
Friends within the neighborhood	42.2 (26)	42.2 (26)	27.1 (22)	50.0 (6)	31.7 (22)	37.0 (38)

tends to discount the degree to which his own success was a function of opportunity because so much of what he observes around him indicates a lack of opportunity.

We noted in Chapter Two that the effects of contextual dissonance on friendship patterns were stronger for these solvent old men than for their poor age peers. And here we see that the poor and the solvent react differently to economic dissonance in terms of their image of the class system. For the poor, increasing neighborhood economic dissonance reduces the proportion of closed system responses, while for the solvent it raises the proportion of such responses. As Table 19 shows, this is the case whether the old men are isolated or integrated into the neighborhood. Indeed, for the poor old men there is no essential difference in the proportion of closed system responses, at each level of neighborhood wealth, whether they are isolated or integrated into the neighborhood. But for solvent old men, while the decrease in closed system responses with lessening neighborhood contextual dissonance remains for isolates and those with local friends alike, the decline is sharper for the isolates.

These findings about the image of a closed society and those of Chapter Two about friendship illuminate each other. The lessening of social isolation from friends which these solvent old men experience in wealthier neighborhoods and the concomitant increase in their rate of local friendships are associated with a decline in their conception of the larger society as a closed system (we are here comparing Tables 19 and 4). Or, put another way, the more these solvent old men are isolated and the less integrated they are into their neighborhoods, the more we find that they think of the society as closed. And this phenomenon occurs under conditions of greatest contextual dissonance, in the poorest areas.

But quite a different picture of the relationship between neighborhood economic context, friendship patterns, and the image of the society emerges when we consider the poor old men. As a glance back at Table 4 reveals, the largest proportions of these men are isolated in the richest neighborhoods, and the smallest proportions have friends there, while in the poorest, most contextually consonant neighborhoods these poor old men are least isolated and most integrated into local friendship relations. In contrast to their

solvent age peers, poor old men give the greatest proportion of
closed system responses if they live in those neighborhoods where
they are most involved in social participation and least isolated
from friends—the poorest areas. For poor old men, then, the image
of a closed society emerges most strongly in local settings which tend
to integrate them socially with relatively high frequency, while for
solvent old men the image of a closed society is most prevalent in
local settings which tend to isolate them relatively frequently.

We stated in Chapter Two that the poor are less responsive
than the solvent to the isolating impact of neighborhood economic
contextual dissonance. And there we conjectured that they develop
an orientation which enables them to cope better than their solvent
age peers with the problems of social participation in neighborhoods
where economic dissimilars are prevalent. And we have just noted
that in such neighborhood economic contexts the smallest proportions of these poor old men hold an image of a closed society. We
interpreted this relationship by stating that the evidence of success
apparent in such neighborhoods of the aged poor makes it less likely
that they will think of the society as closed. This situation is in
contrast to that of the solvent old men in the most economically
dissimilar neighborhoods, where the presence of the poor may contribute to an image of a closed society since the evidence of failure
is most clear there.

Without attempting to address the separate question of
causal priority—Does the conception of the larger society influence
the rate of isolation or does the rate of isolation play a role in forming the conception of the society?—we may make certain inferences
about the particular pattern of attitude and interaction. The impact
of economic differences ought to weigh less heavily on people who
can see dissimilarities of wealth between themselves and their neighbors in a positive light—that is, on those who can look favorably
upon others whose economic standing is different in the sense either
that they are to be admired as persons or that they exemplify a
cultural ideal or norm. In this situation, increasing differences between an individual's wealth and that of his neighbors may not
hamper or deter social affiliation to as great an extent as it may
where such economic differences are viewed negatively—in a situa-

tion, for instance, in which a person has to affiliate with others who cannot be admired as individuals or who exemplify something less than a cultural ideal. This view would appear to be consonant with the data of Chapter Two on friendship patterns and with the findings presented in Table 19. The lesser responsiveness of the aged poor to the isolating effects of economic contextual dissonance occurs in a cultural climate where affiliation with others whose economic standing differs from their own minimizes the beliefs of these men that the system through which they have arrived at old age in poverty is indeed closed. Thus, the isolation effects of neighborhood economic dissonance are somewhat dampened for the poor in comparison to the solvent because dissonant social environments, although inimical in themselves to high rates of friendship, nevertheless, in the case of the poor, hold out the possibility of association with neighbors whose economic status is culturally sanctioned in a positive sense. But solvent old men who form friendships with their neighbors in dissonant neighborhood contexts stand a greater chance of associating with failures. For them, both the cultural sanctions and the surrounding social structure work in the same direction: to increase disaffiliation. Hence we find greater responsiveness of solvent than of poor old men to neighborhood economic structural contexts. And where solvent old working class men are implicated in dissonant economic contexts, whether or not they interact with their neighbors, the proportion of closed system responses they give is relatively high, as high as that found among poor men who live in poor neighborhoods. This suggests that self-stigmatization may be avoided in dissonant neighborhood contexts by solvent old men through low rates of friendship formation there.

NEIGHBORHOOD AGE CONTEXT

As we saw in Chapter Three, poor neighborhoods are highly likely to be populated by older residents. Unfortunately a small case base prevents us from controlling for the wealth of the neighborhoods populated by the old and the young while examining the relationship between friendship patterns and the image of the closed society. But it is still fruitful to assess the relation between the age of the neighborhood, considered as an aggregate characteristic, and the image of the closed society, in order to determine whether it resembles what we have just observed in our consideration of neighborhood wealth.

Strong similarities exist between the relation of images of the closed society and neighborhood age structure and economic structure. For old poor men who are integrated into their neighborhoods, the proportion of closed system responses rises from 19 per cent in the areas with the youngest people to 45 per cent in areas with the oldest people. This relation is the analogue of what we observed above in Table 19, where closed system responses were proportionately most frequent in the poorest areas—the neighborhoods with the oldest people being the poorest areas. For solvent old men with friends in the local area, proportionately more closed system responses, 70 as compared with 40 per cent, are elicited in the neighborhoods with the oldest than in those with the youngest people. (Also, a reverse distribution of closed system responses in age and economic contexts exists for the younger men. The proportions of closed system responses are highest for both poor and solvent younger men in the neighborhoods with the youngest people—as they are also in the wealthiest neighborhoods.) The only difference between economic and age contexts in the patterning of closed system responses concerns the isolates. For them, whether they are over or under sixty-five, there is no appreciable variation in the proportion of closed system responses they give by the age of the neighborhood.

Since the image of the closed society is not subject to the influence of age contexts for men who are isolated but is subject to the influence of economic contexts even for such men, we infer that the neighborhood economic context is the more pervasive contextual factor affecting attitude toward the class system. Therefore, probably because of the dynamics of economic contrast and similarity between these working class men and their neighbors, the pattern of closed society images, just discussed, comes about. It is unlikely that age and age contextual consonance lead to the economic contextual effects on the image of the closed society. However, for the working class men who are active participants in the social life of their neighborhoods, the image of the closed society predominates when they are involved with friends in a local setting where their age and that of their neighbors are similar. And the implication of this phenomenon remains: For old men, the presence of the aged in the local environment is associated with a closed class system (as was the presence of the poor); for younger men, the presence of younger people in the local environment is associated with a closed class system. Members of a given age category associate their own age status with the restrictiveness of the system of economic opportunity if they participate in age-consonant social systems. Disaffection with democratic ideology, it would appear, may be tied to an age cohort substratum among the socially active male members of the working class—most probably as a result of economic contextual phenomena of the kind discussed in the preceding section.

CONCLUSION

In this chapter we have traced some of the linkages among our respondents' beliefs about the class system, their economic history, and their friendship patterns in neighborhoods of varying degrees of wealth and age. We concentrated on the image, held by working class breadwinners, of the closed society. This image, as reflected in our respondents' views about their own advancement, is most prevalent among poor breadwinners with declining incomes over most of their working years. But also, solvent breadwinners whose incomes have failed to keep pace with the rising cost of living since 1935 or else have declined in absolute terms hold an image of the closed society relatively frequently. When asked to consider the future of opportunity for working class people, however, an overwhelming majority of all breadwinners, no matter what path their own income history has taken, conceive of the class system as closed. A major component of these views of the nature of the class system of the future is a belief that automation will prevent advancement and also, to a slightly lesser degree, that educational opportunities will be inadequate for the working class.

The younger breadwinners, those still in the labor force, have the largest proportions of images of a closed class system when asked about their own careers. But when the breadwinners are asked about the future chances for working class people to get ahead, it is, by and large, the older, retired, among them who are pessimistic and who most frequently hold an image of the closed society. Those still in the labor force are in general most disenchanted with democratic ideology, and those who have completed their careers are most pessimistic about the future.

When we considered the relation of neighborhood economic context to our respondents' conceptions of the class system, we found that for old men (no matter what their own income level or their relationship to their neighbors), living in the poorest neighborhoods is associated with holding an image of a closed class system. However, younger working class men seem to be influenced by the neighborhood economic context only if they maintain friendships in the local area. And when they do affiliate with neighbors, it is in the wealthiest, rather than in the poorest, neighborhoods that they most frequently view the class system as closed.

The relationship between neighborhood age structure and the image of the closed society derives from that found when the wealth of the neighborhood was analyzed. Since the oldest areas are also the poorest areas, the patterns observed for the context of neighborhood wealth translate themselves into those for the context of neighborhood age according to this formula.

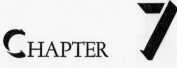

CHAPTER 7

Working Class Social Participation

The Aethiop saith that his Gods are snub-nosed and black, the Thracian that his have blue eyes and red hair.

XENOPHANES

185

At the beginning of this study we posed a heuristic dilemma about conceptions of social isolation. From the stratification tradition of research we identified a point of view which links withdrawal from social relations with low socioeconomic standing. From the gerontological tradition of research we identified two related orientations concerning aging. One claims that isolation stems from the erosion of the structural basis of the authority of the aged and, in combination with this, from the loss of status and role accompanying aging. Another posits the disengagement of the aging person in the form of a mutual withdrawal of the individual and society and asserts that this is an intrinsic life-cycle development with correlates on the level of personality.

Were we now to evaluate these traditional orientations to the problem of social isolation on the basis of the preceding chapters, perhaps we would be forced to conclude that elements of the stratification approach are more fruitful than those of the gerontological approach. However, as the epigraphical fragment above implies, this would serve little better purpose than trying to describe the gods by skin or eye color while neglecting to define them by their divinity. We have found that at all levels, within the portion of the socioeconomic hierarchy we examined, neighborhood contextual dissonance isolates people from friends. Although socioeconomic rank dictates the differential response made to a given neighborhood context and age signifies a role transition from breadwinner to neighbor which sensitizes a person to the influence of the neighborhood context, nevertheless, in themselves, age and rank have no direct relation to isolation from friends. And neither age nor socioeconomic rank in themselves restrict a person's contact with kin. It is a history of economic deprivation which does that along with disrupted family arrangements.

These findings indicate the need for a theoretical orientation toward working class participation in primary relationships which encompasses both traditions of inquiry. This brief concluding chapter would hardly be the place to present such a theory, even were one at hand. But it is appropriate here to call attention to some

186

substantive and theoretical issues raised by our findings, issues which suggest promising paths of exploration toward the goal of a synthesizing conceptual scheme.

The results of our contextual analysis point to the need for an adequate theory of alienation in the working class. Blum (1964)' has called for further research into the role structure of social networks of kin and their bearing upon withdrawal from primary relationships of both the kinship and friendship variety. Although recognizing the potential fruitfulness of such an approach, we prefer to take another line of attack on the problem of working class social isolation and through it return to the question of the relation between kinship and friendship later in this chapter.

The influence on friendship relations of different kinds of social contexts is not uniform at all socioeconomic ranks within the working class. The responsiveness of the solvent to class-linked context and the responsiveness of the poor to family-cycle contexts unrelated to the class structure of the neighborhood suggest that in important respects different levels within the working class may be articulated into alternate social subsystems of primary participation. Our information about the image of the closed society tends to support this thesis. The social participation of the poor and the circumstances under which relatively many of them hold an image of a closed class system lead us to reject as simplistic theories of withdrawal in the sense of apathy. Nonsocioeconomic contexts related to family-cycle operate on the friendship patterns of the poor with considerable power, which indicates a distinctive orientation, not the lack of one. The poor, in contrast to the solvent, adhere to an alternative orientation toward the open nature of the class system which is anchored partly in a history of economic deprivation and which most likely also stems in part from their greater responsiveness to the family-cycle aspects of their local environment. On these grounds, for instance, it is possible to view the solvent who live in poor neighborhoods as adherents of cultural orthodoxy living among dissenters: They may accept a view of the class system as open while the bulk of their neighbors may not. They may adhere to the modal ideology of the society yet find they are in an ideological minority in their particular neighborhood. The orthodox who find themselves surrounded by unbelievers may find social participation with their neighbors more difficult than do those who hold an alternate view but who are also in the minority with respect to their neighbors' ideological perspectives.

One mechanism by which solidarity may come about among the poor was hinted at earlier, in our analysis of age status homophily. We found that in one age cohort at least, the poor more than the solvent had age homophilous relationships. There we alluded to this finding as an indication that the poor were less venturesome and sought less variety in their interpersonal relations than did the solvent. Looking at the same matter from a broader perspective, however, we may also interpret it as an indication of the solidarity of an ideologically heterodox subgroup. We suspect, furthermore, that had it been possible to examine other homophilies, we might have revealed that the poor engage in homophilous pairings over a wide range of characteristics to a greater extent than do the solvent.

A more adequate theoretical model of the transition to old age is also needed for a better understanding of the contextual effects on isolation. The influence of structural contexts on friendship relations is most pronounced after sixty-five, and in some cases it is nonexistent before that age. Furthermore, structural constraints exert their influence chiefly among men. The transition from the role of breadwinner to that of neighbor appears to be a precondition for the operation of several neighborhood structural contexts on working class friendship relations. The orderliness with which structural contexts pattern isolation and friendship leads us to attribute the failure of working class people to have friends to contextual constraints and not to cultural definitions of old age. Yet many observers of the aged claim that the postretirement years are a period intrinsically devoid of age-specific roles. Clearly, further study is required of the role of neighbor as a sequel to the role of breadwinner among aged working class men, both poor and solvent. In particular, it is necessary to describe the dynamics of the transition from breadwinner to neighbor in different neighborhood settings on the part of people who have had differing degrees of economic success as wage earners. A cross-sectional study such as this one does not provide such a description, even though it is possible to distinguish age cohorts in the sample. The description of role transition demands a panel study.

We have seen that restricted kin contact is a characteristic of people with a history of economic deprivation but that their kin networks may be more solidary than are those of people with a greater degree of interaction with relatives. Furthermore, we have noted that kinship and friendship interaction rates are, in the aggregate, apparently unrelated to each other. Yet we would not wish to imply that a connection between kinship and friendship networks is nonexistent, although it may have little to do with frequency of interaction. In both subsystems of social interaction, the immediate neighborhood is a site of intensive relationships. Moreover, the poor, including those who have always been deprived, are more solidary with kin and are more responsive to nonsocioeconomic neighborhood factors. It is worth exploring the possibility that for some segments of the working class population kinship relations serve as mediators or catalysts of friendship relations. If kin reside in the neighborhood, then friends may be met or friendships may be sustained through relatives. This may be easier for the poor than for the solvent precisely because of their more solidary kinship relations, their relative immunity to neighborhood contextual dissonance associated with socioeconomic factors, and their greater responsiveness to non-class–related neighborhood contexts. Further, if the poor represent a relatively solidary enclave, then one means by which its internal bonds are strengthened may be through the utilization of family relations to maintain friendship relations.

Thus we have returned, it will be recognized, to the issue raised at the outset of this chapter—the interpenetration of kinship and friendship networks and how to account for working class primary relationships in both these spheres in a unitary way. We have done so by speculating on the sources of the putative solidarity of the poor within the working class. In the course of these remarks and in the analyses of the preceding chapters which led to them, we have found it necessary to employ concepts which in spite of a difference in language resemble in substance some of those found useful by Blum. In concluding this work, then, it may be profitable to pose some of the common concerns brought to the fore in our contrasting approaches to the problem of variations in kinship and friendship relations as aspects of a general mode of working class social participation. We summarize Blum's approach first.

Blum hinges his theoretical analysis on the notion that working class social participation is a function of the close-knit nature of the social network. By this he means that a working class person's circle of affiliations is structurally undifferentiated—that is, the number of different statuses in the social network is few and the degree of difference among them is small. In such a social network there is no hierarchy of authority and responsibility is decentralized; in consequence the norms of the system may be invoked by any of its members. The integrity of such a social network is maintained by avoiding contact with others who are different since persons with different characteristics from one's own are likely to involve one in cross-pressuring situations. Presumably what is meant here is that visibility is high among members of close-knit networks, and because of the diffusion of authority, sanctions are easily imposed for repeated association with persons who are different. Thus, the working class person is likely to minimize his association with different others and, thereby, to increase his isolation from all but the members of his close-knit circle. This rationale is offered to account for the insulation of working class families and for the isolation of working class people from varied social relationships. Thus the problem of working class alienation is seen by Blum as paradoxical in that it is a function of "intense primary involvement within one's network" of relatively homogeneous peers, which may consist in kin or friends, but most probably both. The question of whether the members of the close-knit network know each other is begged in this view, and in any case it is not clear how it is essential to the argument as developed by Blum. Cross-pressuring situations may be reacted to either by members of the close-knit network as a group or by individual sanctioning of the person under cross-pressure. Since authority is diffuse, sanctions would be equally effective whether applied in concert or by one member of the network acting alone.[1]

[1] There are further difficulties with Blum's approach. For instance, it may be argued that the diffusion of authority among members of a close-knit network who happened to be kin is unlikely since family authority is often centralized. At any rate, this is an empirical question; it could be determined whether kindred who happen to belong to the same social network have equal family authority. One can think of possible genealogical combinations which would permit this.

By contrast, we have barely looked at the internal structure of social networks but instead have approached the problem of social participation and isolation chiefly from the point of view of the constraints imposed on the viability of social circles by external factors. (Our examination of homophily did, however, touch on the composition of the social network.) And for purposes of our analysis, friends and kin were considered separately. Keeping in mind these differences in approach, we see that the implied rationale which emerges from the present study is that the viability of working class social networks is a function of opportunity structure and not internal composition. Association among members of a social network or between members and nonmembers is parsimoniously thought of as a function of contextual dissonance. Association with those who possess different characteristics or similar characteristics, role set heterophily or homophily, is as far as we can ascertain proportional to the local supply of similars. However, where we do find variation in homophily, between the poor and the solvent, we interpret it, most broadly, as a mainfestation of the solidarity obtaining in an alternate social and cultural subsystem. Here we come closest to a common ground with Blum. For him, close-knit networks are homogeneous, as we have found the friends of the poor in a certain age cohort. However, the poor also have more older friends than do the solvent, a fact which is contrary to what we might expect on Blum's view but explicable under our interpretation, given in Chapter Four. In any case, whether the internal dynamics of close-knit networks impose status homophily on members or whether homophily is a function of external opportunity may not be mutually exclusive considerations. Once social networks are better understood, we may see that these are mutually reinforcing processes.

But there is a prior question to be answered by further study, a question which may expand our knowledge of the relationship between internal and external factors affecting the nature of social networks. Does the presence of kin who know or interact with the friends of a working class person affect the characteristics of his social network? Here differences within the working class between the poor and the solvent and between the working and middle class may be considerable. The presence of kin in the neighborhood may be as important a factor in isolation from friends as contextual dissonance is. Where kin live in the neighborhood and are the friends of our respondents' friends, moreover, they may be influential in determining the distribution of authority and responsibility within the network of social participation.

In this chapter we have attempted to clarify some of the theoretical issues confronting those who would interrelate social structure and social class to the patterning of primary relationships. We have considered as a foil to our perspective Blum's stimulating and imaginative attempt at a theoretical synthesis through his use of the social network concept to reinterpret conventional sociological views of working class social life. By posing the issues differently and making interpretations somewhat at variance with his, we have tried to inspire fruitful empirical and theoretical investigation in this much studied but still only partly understood area.

Bibliography

ADAMS, B. N. *Kinship in an Urban Setting*. Chicago: Markham, 1968.

AXELROD, M. "Urban Structure and Social Participation." *American Sociological Review*, 1956, *21*, 13–18.

AXELROD, M., AND SHARP, H. "Mutual Aid Among Relatives in Urban Populations." In R. Freedman et al., *Principles of Sociology*. New York: Holt, 1956.

BARRON, M. *The Aging American*. New York: Crowell, 1961.

BELL, W. "Anomie, Social Isolation and the Class Structure." *Sociometry*, 1957, *20*, 105–16.

BELL, W. "The Utility of the Shevky Typology for the Design of Urban Sub-Area Field Studies." In G. A. Theodoreson (Ed.), *Studies in Human Ecology*. Evanston: Row, Peterson, 1961.

BELL, W., AND BOAT, M. D. "Urban Neighborhoods and Informal Social Relations." *American Journal of Sociology*, 1957, *62*, 391–98.

BELL, W., AND FORCE, M. T. "Urban Neighborhood Types and Participation in Formal Associations." *American Sociological Review*, 1956, *21*, 25–34.

BLAU, Z. "Structural Constraints on Friendships in Old Age." *American Sociological Review*, 1961, *26*, 429–39.

BLUM, A. F. "Social Structure, Social Class, and Participation in Primary Relationships." In A. Shostak and W. Gomberg (Eds.), *Blue-Collar World: Studies of the American Worker*. Englewood Cliffs: Prentice-Hall, 1964.

BOOTH, C. *Life and Labour of the People in London*. London: Macmillan, 1892.

BURCHINAL, L. "The Premarital Dyad and Love Involvement." In H. T. Christensen (Ed.), *Handbook of Marriage and the Family*. Chicago: Rand McNally, 1964.

COHEN, A. K., AND HODGES, H. M., JR. "Characteristics of the Lower-Blue-Collar-Class." *Social Problems*, 1963, *10*, 303–334.

CUMMING, E., DEAN, L. R., NEWELL, D. S., AND MCCAFFREY, I. "Disengagement: A Tentative Theory of Aging." *Sociometry*, 1960, *23*, 23–35.

CUMMING, E., AND HENRY, W. E. *Growing Old: The Process of Disengagement*. New York: Basic Books, 1961.

CUMMING, E., AND SCHNEIDER, D. M. "Sibling Solidarity: A Property of American Kinship." *American Anthropologist*, 1961, *63*, 498–507.

DEAN, L. "Aging and the Decline of Affect." *Journal of Gerontology*, 1962, *17*, 440–46.

DOTSON, F. "Patterns of Voluntary Association Among Urban Working Class Families." *American Sociological Review*, 1951, *16*, 687–93.

DUBIN, R. "Industrial Workers' Worlds: A Study of the 'Central

Life Interests' of Industrial Workers." *Social Problems,* 1956, *3,* 131–42.

FARBER, B. "Kinship Laterality and the Emotionally Disturbed Child." In B. Farber (Ed.), *Kinship and Family Organization.* New York: Wiley, 1966.

FIRTH, R. (Ed.) *Two Studies of Kinship in London.* London School of Economics Monographs on Social Anthropology, No. 15. London: Athlone Press, 1950.

FOX, R. *Kinship and Marriage: An Anthropological Perspective.* London: Nicholls, 1967.

FREEMAN, J. D. "On the Concept of the Kindred." *Journal of the Royal Anthropological Institute,* 1961, *91,* 192–220.

GANS, H. J. *The Urban Villagers: Group and Class in the Life of Italian-Americans.* New York: Free Press, 1962.

GREER, S. "Urbanism Reconsidered: A Comparative Study of Local Areas in a Metropolis." *American Sociological Review,* 1956, *21,* 19–25.

HODGES, H. M., JR. *Social Stratification: Class in America.* Cambridge: Schenkman, 1964.

HOGGART, R. *The Uses of Literacy: Changing Patterns in English Mass Culture.* Fairlawn: Essential Books, 1957.

HOLLINGSHEAD, A. B. "Class Differences in Family Stability." In M. B. Sussman (Ed.), *Sourcebook in Marriage and the Family.* New York: Houghton Mifflin, 1955.

HOMANS, G. C., AND SCHNEIDER, D. M. "Kinship Terminology and the American Kinship System." *American Anthropologist,* 1955, *57,* 1194–1208.

KAHL, J. A. *The American Class Structure.* New York: Rinehart, 1957.

KAPLAN, S. "Old Age Assistance: Children's Contributions to Aged Parents." *Social Security Bulletin,* 1957, *20,* 3–8.

KNUPFER, G. "Portrait of the Underdog." *The Public Opinion Quarterly,* 1947, *11,* 103–14.

KOMAROVSKY, M. *Blue-Collar Marriage.* New York: Random House, 1962.

KRIESBERG, L., AND BELLIN, S. S. *Fatherless Families and Housing: A Study of Dependency.* Washington, D.C.: Report to the Welfare Administration, U.S. Department of Health, Education, and Welfare, 1965.

KUTNER, B., FANSHEL, D., TOGO, A. M., AND LANGNER, T. S. *Five Hundred Over Sixty.* New York: Russell Sage Foundation, 1956.

LANCASTER, L. "Some Conceptual Problems in the Study of Family and Kin Ties in the British Isles." *British Journal of Sociology,* 1961, *12,* 317–32.

LAZARSFELD, P. F., AND MERTON, R. K. "Friendship as Social Process: A Substantive and Methodological Analysis." In M. Berger

(Ed.), *Freedom and Control in Modern Society*. New York: Van Nostrand, 1954.

LEICHTER, H. J., AND ROGERS, C. Unpublished manuscript cited in W. J. Goode, *World Revolution and Family Patterns*. New York: Free Press, 1963. P. 72.

LEVY, M. J., AND FALLERS, L. A. "The Family: Some Comparative Considerations." *American Anthropologist*, 1959, *61*, 647–51.

LITWAK, E. "The Use of Extended Family Groups in the Achievement of Social Goals: Some Policy Implications." *Social Problems*, 1959, *7*, 177–87.

LITWAK, E. "Occupational Mobility and Extended Family Cohesion." *American Sociological Review*, 1960, *25*, 9–20. (a)

LITWAK, E. "Geographical Mobility and Extended Family Cohesion." *American Sociological Review*, 1960, *25*, 385–94. (b)

LOWENTHAL, M. F. "Social Isolation and Mental Illness in Old Age." *American Sociological Review*, 1964, *29*, 54–70.

LOWENTHAL, M. F., BERKMAN, P. L., AND ASSOCIATES. *Aging and Mental Disorder in San Francisco: A Social Psychiatric Study*. San Francisco: Jossey-Bass, 1967.

MCGOUGH, D. M. *Social Factor Analysis: Technical Report No. 11*. Philadelphia: Health and Welfare Council, Community Renewal Program of Philadelphia, 1964.

MERTON, R. K. *Social Theory and Social Structure*. Glencoe: Free Press, 1957.

MITCHELL, W. E. "Theoretical Problems in the Concept of the Kindred." *American Anthropologist*, 1963, *65*, 343–54.

MURDOCK, G. P. *Social Structure*. New York: Free Press, 1949.

NEW YORK STATE DIVISION OF HOUSING. "Housing Problems and Preferences of Aging Persons on the Site of Borgia Butler Houses." Mimeographed, 1958.

PALMER, G. *Philadelphia Workers in a Changing Economy*. Philadelphia: University of Pennsylvania Press, 1956.

PARSONS, T. "The Kinship System of the Contemporary United States." *American Anthropologist*, 1943, *45*, 22–38.

PARSONS, T. *The Social System*. Glencoe: Free Press, 1951.

PITTS, J. R. *"The Structural-Functional Approach."* In H. T. Christensen (Ed.), *Handbook of Marriage and the Family*. Chicago: Rand McNally, 1964.

POPE, H. "Economic Deprivation and Social Participation in a Group of 'Middle Class' Factory Workers." *Social Problems*, 1964, *11*, 290–300.

QUERY, W. T. *Illness, Work, and Poverty*. San Francisco: Jossey-Bass, 1968.

ROBINS, L. N., AND TOMANEC, M. "Closeness to Blood Relatives Outside the Immediate Family." *Marriage and Family Living*, 1962, *24*, 340–46.

ROSE, A. "The Subculture of the Aging: A Framework for Research in Social Gerontology." In A. Rose and W. Peterson (Eds.), *Older People and Their Social World*. Philadelphia: Davis, 1965.

ROSENBERG, M. "The Dissonant Religious Context and Emotional Disturbance." *American Journal of Sociology*, 1962, *68*, 1–10.

ROSOW, I. "Old Age: One Moral Dilemma of an Affluent Society." *The Gerontologist*, 1962, 2, 182–91.

ROSOW, I. *Social Integration of the Aged*. New York: Free Press, 1967.

SCHNEIDER, D. M. *American Kinship: A Cultural Account*. Englewood Cliffs: Prentice-Hall, 1968.

SCHORR, A. *Filial Responsibility in the Modern American Family*. Washington, D.C.: Social Security Administration, 1960.

SHANAS, E. "Family Responsibility and the Health of Older People." *Journal of Gerontology*, 1960, *15*, 408–11.

SHANAS, E. *Family Relationships of Older People*. New York: Health Information Foundation Research Series 20, 1961. (a)

SHANAS, E. "Living Arrangements of Older People in the United States." *The Gerontologist*, 1961, *1*, 27–29. (b)

SHANAS, E., AND STREIB, G. F. (Eds.) *Social Structure and the Family: Generational Relationships*. Englewood Cliffs: Prentice-Hall, 1965.

SMITH, J., FORM, W., AND STONE, G. "Local Intimacy in a Middle-sized City." *American Journal of Sociology*, 1954, *60*, 276–84.

STONE, C., AND SLOCUM, W. *A Look a Thurston County's Older People*. Pullman, Washington: Washington Agricultural Experimental Stations, Bulletin 573, State College of Washington, 1957.

STOTLAND, E. *The Psychology of Hope*. San Francisco: Jossey-Bass, 1969.

SURVEY RESEARCH CENTER. *A Social Profile of Detroit, 1956*. Ann Arbor: University of Michigan, 1957.

SUSSMAN, M. B. "The Help Pattern in the Middle Class Family." *American Sociological Review*, 1953, *18*, 22–28.

SUSSMAN, M. B. "The Isolated Nuclear Family: Fact or Fiction." *Social Problems*, 1959, *6*, 333–40.

SUSSMAN, M. B., AND BURCHINAL, L. "Kin Family Network: Unheralded Structure in Current Conceptualizations of Family Functioning." *Marriage and Family Living*, 1962, *24*, 231–40.

TOWNSEND, P. *Family Life of Old People*. London: Routledge and Kegan Paul, 1957.

UNITED STATES BUREAU OF THE CENSUS. *U.S. Census of Population and Housing: 1960.* Census Tracts. Final Report PHC (1)-116. Washington, D.C.: U.S. Government Printing Office, 1962.

WEBBER, I. L. "The Organized Social Life of the Retired: Two Florida Communities." *American Journal of Sociology,* 1954, *59,* 340–46.

WEBER, M. *Economy and Society.* New York: Bedminster Press, 1968.

WHYTE, W. F. *Street Corner Society: The Social Structure of an Italian Slum.* Chicago: University of Chicago Press, 1943.

WILENSKY, H. L. "Orderly Careers and Social Participation: The Impact of Work History on Social Integration in the Middle Mass." *American Sociological Review,* 1961, *26,* 521–39.

WILLMOTT, P., AND YOUNG, M. *Family and Class in a London Suburb.* London: Routledge and Kegan Paul, 1960.

YOUNG, M., AND GEERTZ, H. "Old Age in London and San Francisco: Some Families Compared." *British Journal of Sociology,* 1961, *12,* 124–41.

YOUNG, M., AND WILLMOTT, P. *Family and Kinship in East London.* Baltimore: Penguin Books, 1957.

Index

199

63–65; increasing mean age in, 92; and isolation from friends, 59–71; and old wives, 62, 65; and older friends, 101–102; in oldest neighborhoods, reversal of friendship patterns in, 63, 67, 70–71; and social evaluation of old age, 68–69; strength and direction of, 60; and structured opportunity for friendship, 102

Structural contexts, income: consonance and dissonance in, 31, 36, 37–41, 182; effects of on older women, 39–40; and isolation from friends, 36–43; and younger men and women, 41

Structural contexts, marital: and isolation from friends, 71–73; and marital status of respondents, 71–72; and retirement, 71–72

Structural contexts, occupational: consonant labor force, 44, 45; consonant blue collar, 45, 46; and differential impact on poor and solvent old men, 44, 45; effects of consonance and dissonance in, 47, 48; indicators of, 44; and isolation from friends, 43–50

Structural contexts, racial: dissonance in, 53; and isolation from friends, 50–53, 79, 80

Structural contexts, socially reproductive: elements of, 79–80; and family-cycle contexts, 79–80; and isolation from friends, 77–81; and neighborhood wealth, 79; and socially non-

reproductive, 77; and status homophily, 88

SUSSMAN, M. B., 4, 5, 113, 114

T

TOGO, A. M., 7n
TOMANEC, M., 122
TOWNSEND, P., 2, 5

U

Unemployment: and rate of contact with kin, 136–137; rates of in sample, 21; and self-confidence in social interaction, 136

Universe of kin, concept of, 141. *See also* Kin; Kinship

U. S. Bureau of the Census, 19–20

V

Value homophily, 32
Visibility of the old, 2

W

WEBBER, I. L., 31
WEBER, M., 57, 89
WHYTE, W. F., 29, 30
WILENSKY, H. L., 128, 137
WILMOTT, P., 4, 30, 32, 121
Withdrawal of the aged, 92; as life-cycle development, 2, 186; and low self-esteem, 136; low status as a precondition for, 29; theories about, 149, 153, 187

Women, contextual effects on friendships of, 40, 41, 60, 65

Y

YOUNG, M., 4, 5, 30, 32, 121